MR. PEPYS AND MR. EVELYN

From JOHN EVELYN *To* SAMUEL PEPYS
"I send you, Sir, my face, such as it was of *yore*,
but is now *no more* (*tanto mutata*)"

Mr. PEPYS

AND

Mr. EVELYN

by CLARA MARBURG Kirk

PHILADELPHIA:

University of Pennsylvania Press

London
Humphrey Milford
Oxford University Press

MCMXXXV

Copyright 1935
UNIVERSITY OF PENNSYLVANIA PRESS
Manufactured in the United States of America

THE DESIGN ON THE FRONT COVER
REPRESENTS THE ARMS OF JOHN EVELYN

TO
Rudolf Kirk

Preface

A GRANT from the American Council of Learned Societies made it possible for me to spend the summer of 1933 in England in pursuit of Pepys and Evelyn letters. I am glad to have this opportunity to thank the Council for its generosity. I wish also to thank Dr. A. S. W. Rosenbach of Philadelphia, the Master and Fellows of Magdalene College, Cambridge, the librarians of the Bodleian, Henry E. Huntington, and Morgan libraries, the authorities of the British Museum, the Pennsylvania Historical Society, and the Public Record Office, for permission to print manuscripts from their collections. It is necessary to include in the Appendix the name of a private collector who would not allow me to study his Pepys-Evelyn letters.

I should like to thank the several friends, especially Miss Lucy M. Donnelly and Dr. Samuel C. Chew of Bryn Mawr College, who read and corrected my manuscript. Dr. C. M. Hall of Rutgers University was of great assistance to me in deciphering Evelyn's inaccurate Greek and Latin phrases. Dr. F. E. Bowman of the University of Rochester generously drew my attention to a number of letters which would otherwise have been omitted. Mr. Francis McD. C. Turner, the Pepysian Librarian, smoothed the way for me in my use of the Bibliotheca Pepysiana. Mr. Edwin Chappell transcribed a shorthand letter for me. It is perhaps not necessary to say that I was helped at every stage in compiling this book by my husband, Dr. Rudolf Kirk, of Rutgers University, who turned the task of collecting and editing these letters into a pleasure.

C. M.

June 1, 1935

Contents

	page
PREFACE	vii
INTRODUCING MR. PEPYS AND MR. EVELYN	1
CHAPTER I: PUBLICK EMPLOYMENT	5
CHAPTER II: PRIVATE ENJOYMENT	39
NOTES	75
APPENDIX	83
I. Manuscript Letters	84
Pepys-Evelyn	
Hewer-Evelyn	
Jackson-Evelyn	
II. Finding List of Letters Advertised in Book Catalogues	146
III. Finding List of Printed Letters	153

Illustrations

PORTRAITS OF JOHN EVELYN AND SAMUEL PEPYS
From the Bibliotheca Pepysiana *frontispiece*

LETTER FROM JOHN EVELYN TO SAMUEL PEPYS,
September 23, 1665 *facing page* 8

LETTER FROM SAMUEL PEPYS TO JOHN EVELYN,
February 15, 1695 *facing page* 60

Introducing
Mr. Pepys and Mr. Evelyn

At noon all of us dined at Captain Cocke's at a good chine of beef, and other good meat; but, being all frost-bitten, was most of it unroast; but very merry, and a good dish of fowle we dressed ourselves. Mr. Evelyn there, in very good humour. All the afternoon till night pleasant, and then I took my leave of them and to the office, where I wrote my letters, and away home.[1]

THUS wrote Pepys in his Diary on a December evening of 1665, after a long and varied afternoon spent with his fellow Commissioners for the sick and wounded of the Dutch War. Had we assisted at the dressing of the "good dish of fowle" at Captain Cocke's, would we have taken our leave at last with a somewhat altered impression of the stately and learned Mr. Evelyn, the plain and genial Mr. Pepys?

Though we may not share in this particular piece of frost-bitten meat, and shall have to imagine the conversation which made "all the afternoon till night pleasant," we can by studying the many letters[2] we possess which Pepys and Evelyn exchanged in the course of their forty-year friendship, and by making the most of the numerous encounters described in the Diaries of these busy Londoners,* almost share the dish of tripe in Pepys' back parlor, almost take barge with them to Trinity House in London, there to witness the great dinner, "above 80 at one table," where "Mr. Pepys, Secretary to ye Admiralty, was a second time chosen Master."[3] And by associating in this way with Pepys and Evelyn through many years we may come finally to

---

* Pepys, younger than Evelyn and more impressed by their conversations, referred to Evelyn thirty-six times between March 1, 1665, and March 29, 1669; Evelyn, who made no reference to Pepys during those years, immediately took up the story at the close of Pepys' Diary and described thirty encounters with him from June 10, 1669, until his death in 1703. In May 1683 Pepys alluded to Evelyn again. (*The Tangier Papers of Samuel Pepys,* Edwin Chappell, London, 1935, p. 314)

understand certain sides of their characters which the reading of their separate diaries hardly reveals.

If we are to follow these two friends from 1665 until 1703, we must be prepared for all the chances and changes of the fortunes of two active men in the difficult time of Charles II. We must go with them to the Bell Tavern, there to talk of how to make room for the sick and dying prisoners of the Dutch War; we must take our place in great halls: "I supp'd this night with Mr. Secretary [Pepys]," wrote Evelyn, "at one Mr. Houblon's, a French merchant, who had his house furnish'd *en Prince,* and gave us a splendid entertainment." [4] And finally we must be willing to share disconsolate dinners in the Tower, somewhat cheered by the roast fowl sent by Mr. Evelyn in advance: "I din'd with Mr. Pepys in the Tower, he having ben committed by ye House of Commons for misdemeanours in the Admiralty when he was Secretary." [5]

As one pursues these respectable gentlemen from tavern to hall, and, at last, when they have grown too old for the diversions of London, to their country estates, one comes to feel the amusing contrast between the two, alternately host and guest. Dinners at "Paradisial Clapham," as Evelyn called the country place to which Pepys finally retired, would certainly have made us feel the robust warmheartedness of our host. "I dined to-day . . . at Mr. Pepys," [6] wrote Mr. Wanley, who frequently foregathered with these friends,

who entertained us with that obliging kindness which engages all that he converses with into a love and respect for his person, which time that destroys other things, does digest into a habit, and renders it so perfect that it generally lasts as long as a man's life.

Dinners at Sayes Court, on the other hand, presided over by the exquisite scholar, Mr. Evelyn, would have given us an awed sense of what a "philosophical meal" might be. "The house was low but elegantly set off with ornaments and quaint mottoes," [7] wrote the Lordkeeper of Guilford, after his pilgrimage to Deptford.

. . . above all his garden was exquisite, . . . [the flowers and shrubs] appeared all so thriving and clean, and that in so much variety, no one could be satiated in viewing; and to these were added plenty of ingenious discourses, which made the time short.

It is the "ingenious discourses" of these two men of the world, Mr. Pepys and Mr. Evelyn, which I wish to consider in the following essay. They concern themselves with the affairs of the day. Who is to make room for the sick and wounded seamen of the Dutch War; how shall London be rebuilt after the Great Fire; and what of the dirt on the Temple stairs? But busy though Pepys and Evelyn were with their commissions and committees, their conversations touched, too, on all manner of learning, from the Arundel Marbles, which, through Evelyn's intercessions, were presented to Oxford in 1667, to the smallest morsel of scientific gossip. "Pray know," [8] wrote Pepys in despair to Captain Hatton, "that I am in great want of your help and my friend Mr. Evelyn's . . . how to come at the history of birds' nests, if any such were ever wrott." And finally these conversations, lasting through forty crowded years, turned these aging friends into philosophers, each after his own manner, who took pleasure in sharing their cheese and bacon at the country retreats of Clapham and Deptford, as well as their views of "this despicable molehill on which we mortals crawle, and keepe such a stirr about as if the τὸ πὰν (this *All*) were created for us little vermine." [9]

If one is willing to listen to these varying conversations one emerges at last with a curiously altered picture of both Evelyn and Pepys. For one cannot think of Evelyn as altogether aloof and pedantic if Pepys towards the end of his life could write to him,

Dear Sir, As much as I am (I bless God!) in perfect present ease here, as to my health, 'tis little less, however, than a very burial to me . . . [for I lack] the few old and learned friends I had flattered myself with the hopes of closing the little residue of my life in the continued enjoyment of, and at the head of them all, the most inestimable Mr. Evelyn.[10]

And we cannot think of Pepys as the self-seeking and trivial Londoner only, if Evelyn could write to him,

I inquire not what you do or think but how you do, because I am perswaded we think much alike; I onely wish I could do so too, for I should then be allways doing well.[11]

With such measured politeness Pepys, at the age of sixty-eight wrote to Evelyn, and Evelyn, at eighty-one, to Pepys. While one is refreshed by the unbroken decorum of this seventeenth-century friendship, and absorbed by the unfolding interests which mark its progress, one is also amused by the fact that, for all the dinner parties, council meetings and gossips in Whitehall, we know Pepys in the end better than the ingenuous and high-minded Evelyn ever could. For we have only to look into Pepys' Diary to discover that he passed an hour with Sarah at the Swan before viewing Evelyn's collections of engravings at Deptford, and, what is worse, that he considered Evelyn's poems, which he had just been obliged to hear, "very good, but not as he conceits them, I think, to be."[12] But Pepys was willing to allow for "a little conceitedness" in his unhumorous older friend, whose head was packed with such an assortment of information on coins and shrubberies, hieroglyphics and chemistry. He was shrewd enough to refrain from criticizing Evelyn outside the covers of his Diary, and Evelyn was not sufficiently shrewd to suspect that all of Pepys' hours of leisure were not spent among the virtuosi.

Perhaps it was not a lack of shrewdness, but a certain refined detachment which prevented Evelyn from looking too closely into Pepys' mind. This same detachment holds the modern reader at a polite distance from the real Evelyn, in spite of the detailed and careful Diary, and makes one welcome the opportunity to observe Evelyn at somewhat closer range through the letters which passed between him and his genial friend, Pepys, in the course of so many years. For, with generous admiration on one side, and politeness akin to guilelessness on the other, this friendship grew and prospered without a break from the time when both men were emerging into prominence until their deaths, only three years apart.

CHAPTER ONE

Publick Employment

I

SEPTEMBER 9, 1665, "a most cursed rainy afternoon." And Pepys, "forced to go to the office on foot through all the rain," was wet to the skin and almost spoiled his breeches. But, "At noon, by invitation, to my Lord Bruncker's, all of us, to dinner, where a good venison pasty, and mighty merry." Here were also Sir W. Doily, lately come from Ipswich about the sick and wounded of the Dutch War, and Mr. Evelyn and Captain Cocke, both of them Commissioners for the wounded seamen. But in spite of the good company and the venison pasty at the home of the powerful Lord Brouncker, President of the Navy Board, the day grew only worse as it progressed. "Rained all the afternoon and evening," so that the guests were forced finally to stay to supper at Captain Cocke's. Rain outside; a circle of gloomy faces within. For only discouraging news had come of the English ships which had set sail in July in the hopes of encountering and capturing the Dutch East India ships as they made their circuitous way back to Holland around the coast of Scotland and Norway with their rich freight of cinnamon, nutmeg, silks, and indigo. Though Pepys had little confidence in Captain Cocke's honesty, and still less in the ability of this "greatest epicure in the world," who had "no Logique in his head at all," he was depressed by the news Cocke brought them this evening.

But that that put us into this great melancholy, was the newes brought to-day, which Captain Cocke reports as a certain truth, that all the Dutch fleete, men-of-war and merchant East India ships, are got every one in from Bergen the 3d of this month, Sunday last; which will make us all ridiculous. . . . Full of these melancholy thoughts, to bed; where, though I lay the softest I ever did in my life, with a downe bed, after the Danish manner, upon me, yet I slept very ill.

The news later proved false. But it is not surprising that Pepys should have spent a restless night at Captain Cocke's, for it was his patron and cousin, Lord Sandwich, who commanded the English fleet, the fate of which was then not certainly known.

Though Pepys was but a man of thirty-two at that time, and one who had only recently learned his multiplication tables, he already felt himself coming into prominence. Five years earlier, in 1660, he had been made Clerk of the Acts, Justice of the Peace for Middlesex, Clerk of the Privy Seal, and, in 1664, a member of the Corporation of the Royal Fishery, "So that on all hands, by God's blessing," he found himself "a very rising man."[1] Only a year before he had been selected to straighten out the tangled accounts of the Tangier Commission, which he did so successfully that the Lord Chancellor stroked him on the head, to his infinite satisfaction. He now walked with great confidence among the courtiers of Whitehall, had his crest put on his wine bottles, and noted that the Lord Mayor of London was very respectful to him. "Lord! to see how I am treated, that come from so mean a beginning, is matter of wonder to me."[2]

Lord Sandwich and the fleet were soon anchored in the Thames. Pepys was invited to attend a Council of War on one of the ships, where he was not slow to realize that the welfare of the nation was "committed to very ordinary heads." It had become clear to Pepys, during the summer of 1665, that the system of provisioning the ships under the direction of Dennis Gauden, the Victualler, had been responsible for the repeated ignominious returns of the English fleet, and now Lord Sandwich himself told those gathered to confer with him that he believed "no fleete was ever set to sea in so ill condition of provision, as this was when it went out last."[3] Pepys lost no time in hitting on a plan that he might make "some profit" out of the business, which he hoped "justly to do to the King's advantage."[4] He drew up a "letter by way of discourse" to the Duke of Albemarle, giving his "conception how the business of the Victualling should be ordered," "wherein," he wrote, "I have taken great pains and I think have hitt the right if they will but follow it." [5] On October 14 his proposal, expressed with such clarity and confidence, was read before the King and his advisers, "with complete applause and satisfaction." Pepys was "overjoyed and proud" of the success of his suggestion, "and now," he confessed frankly in his Diary, "my head is full how to make some profit of it to myself or people." [6] Through Mr. Coventry, Pepys transmitted the idea to the Duke of Albemarle that he himself would make a suitable Surveyor General of the victualling business, and accordingly the position was created for him on October 25.

But provisioning the fleet was not the only means by which Pepys hoped to be useful to himself and to the King. Lord Sandwich had brought the prize ships of the Dutch East India company safely to shore, and now planned "to get money, and afterwards to get the King's allowance thereof, it being easier," he observed, "to keepe money when got of the King than to get it when it is too late." [7] In spite of "the craft, and not good condition, it may be, of Captain Cocke," [8] Pepys took him as a partner, and, with Sir Roger Cuttance, bought from Lord Sandwich £5,000 of the treasure from the East, which they hoped to dispose of again for a larger sum. After concealing the prize goods in London lodgings, and buying off one Captain Fisher who came to seize them, Pepys and Cocke did profit by their venture. Indeed, one notices that Pepys profited very handsomely by the events, so inaccurately reported by Captain Cocke on that "cursed rainy afternoon" in September when the disgruntled Commissioners met over their venison pasty.

Evelyn, thirteen years older than Pepys, and well known in London, not only as the author of *An Apology for the Royal Party,* printed in 1659 when it was dangerous to defend the King, but also as Commissioner for Improving the Streets and Buildings of London, and for Regulating Hackney Coaches, listened to the news of this fresh discouragement with less thought of personal gain, and more of the suffering and confusion likely to result from further defeat. For he had the year before been made one of the Commissioners for the Sick and Wounded from the Dutch War, "a very troublesome and sad employment," and one which Evelyn made central in his life for many years to come. He, and his fellow Commissioners, Sir William Doily, Sir Thomas Clifford, and Bullein Theymes, had established themselves in Painters Hall the year before this melancholy September, with clerks, messengers, and, by Evelyn's direction, a motto on their seal, *Fac similiter,* under the figure of the Good Samaritan. Each Commissioner had his district, and for more than twenty years, until he handed in his final report in 1688, we read in Evelyn's Diary of his weary trips from Rochester to Chatham, from Gravesend to Maidstone, in his district of Kent and Surrey, and of his efforts to find ways of providing fuel and clothes as well as food for the seamen and their families. The April before this supper at Captain Cocke's, Evelyn had attended a great dinner at Trinity House, where he had received the second £5,000 for the sick and wounded English seamen and Dutch prisoners. But on May 16 Evelyn had gone to the King in his Council Chamber to tell him that the weekly expense was £1,000. In June he went to His Grace, the Duke of York, and asked for another £20,000, and the use of Savoy Hospital, all of which was granted. "Hence to ye Royal Society," he added, "to refresh among ye philosophers." The weekly cost of relief soon reached £7,000, and Evelyn, who suffered to see the prisoners put "stark naked and mortified on the shore," himself contributed to the work "no inconsiderable sum," which the government never repaid. Though Captain Cocke's false news of defeat stirred Pepys to thoughts of profit it meant only loss to Evelyn.

II

On September 17, the day before Pepys' conversation with Lord Sandwich, which suggested to his resourceful mind how he might thereby find himself "a jobb of work in it," Evelyn had received a letter from Lord Sandwich reporting the defeat of the Dutch, and announcing the arrival of three thousand prisoners which Evelyn must dispose of. "I was exceedingly perplex'd," wrote Evelyn to Pepys. But later in the month his perplexity turned to despair when £3,000 of the £5,000 he was to receive was "diverted" to other purposes. "I am almost in despair," he wrote to Pepys on September 23, "you will pardon the passion of, S^r, y^r most faithful Ser^t

Sayes – Court 23: S: –65

There are divers miserably sick prisoners at Woolwich, especially in this same ship: If they could be convey'd downe to our Fly-boates before Gravesend, Our Chirurgeon there might looke after them; & they have also a Guard; but you know I am prohibited receiving any at Woolwich, even of our owne: they might be, I suppose, at Erith; but how shall we (when recover'd) secure them from running away? At Gravesend we are forc'd to make stay of one of my Flie-boats on purpose, for the numerous sick-prisoners wch we could not march w their fellows to Leeds; therefore I beseech you order them by some meanes or other to be sent (vez the sick onely) to those Vessels at Gravesend, where there will be care taken for them:

Sr, since I saw you yesterday, comes notice to me that of the 5000 lb was to touch afrom Wm Kingdon by order of my Ld: Ashley, no lesse then 3000 lb of it is diverted for other purposes from Oxford: consider w indignation, the misery, & confusion all will be in at Chatham, & Gravesend, where I was threatned to have ye sick all oppos'd, if by Thursday next I did not send them 2000 lb: & in what a condition ye prisoners at Leeds, are like to be: If my Ld: of Albemarle (to whom I am now hasty) do not this day helpe me by an high hand; dreadfull will be ye consequence

LETTER FROM JOHN EVELYN TO SAMUEL PEPYS
September 23, 1665

J Evelyn." [9] Evelyn arrived in person in Pepys' office the same day to find Pepys about to consult with Lord Sandwich as to how to dispose of the noble Dutch merchant ships to their mutual advantage. "I advised him not to trust Cocke too far, and did therefore offer him ready money for a £1,000 or two, which he listens to and do agree to, which is great joy to me, hoping thereby to get something!" [10] Pepys was not slow to see the connection between Evelyn's appeal for his suffering men and the government's need for ready money in exchange for the perplexing prize ships. "Thence by coach to Lambeth," he continued the story in his Diary,

his Lordship, and all our office, and Mr. Evelyn, to the Duke of Albemarle, where, after the compliment with my Lord very kind, we sat down to consult of the disposing and supporting of the fleete with victuals and money, and for the sick men and prisoners; and I did propose the taking out some goods out of the prizes, to the value of £10,000, which was accorded to, and an order, drawn up and signed by the Duke and my Lord, done in the best manner I can, and referred to my Lord Bruncker and Sir J. Minnes, but what inconveniences may arise from it I do not yet see, but fear there may be many. Here we dined.

The "inconveniences," which finally brought about Lord Sandwich's fall, were many, not the least of them being the fact that Evelyn did not get the necessary money. Six days after this dinner with the Duke of Albemarle, on September 29, Evelyn sent to Pepys a personal messenger to describe the "extreamist misery of both our owne & prisoners, for want of bread to prevent them from perishing," [11] and the following day wrote a detailed report for Pepys to submit to those in authority, in which he said, "I cannot do miracles, nor know I how to sell goods & treate wth the Merchants. . . . But I am at all moments ready (in accknowledgemete of these deficiencys,) to resigne the hono^r his Matie has don me." [12]

Perhaps it was this letter from Evelyn which moved Pepys to describe in his Diary on that same day the "poor wretches," "lying before our office doors all night and all day. . . . God remove this difficulty!" he sighed, on his way to a dinner party which he described as "mighty merry," except for the fact that as he left the house he was "set upon" by these same "poor wretches," whom he "did give good words and some little money to, and the poor people went away like lambs." Pepys was troubled and perplexed "to the heart" by the seamen that lay starving in the streets "for lack of money," but it was Evelyn who gave all of his time to soliciting for money to keep his "miserable flock from perishing."

For the remainder of that year and well into the next, Evelyn's "earnest entreaties" kept Pepys uncomfortably aware of the suffering which he was inclined to overlook. Without money, Evelyn reminded him, he could not feed several thousand prisoners, though he was working night and day to turn Leeds Castle and Chelsea College into hospitals. It was not his duty to provide money, he said, but to dispense it when he had it. Evelyn, already aware of Pepys' "personal civilities" towards him, was loath to trouble him with his "impertinencies," and would not do so were the situation less desperate. Would Pepys not refresh himself in Evelyn's "poore Garden" when he had "best leasure," and there give him commands as to how to arrange for his "miserable creatures"?

It was Evelyn, and not Pepys, who made a real attempt to alleviate the suffering of the disabled soldiers. On January 31, Evelyn sent Pepys his "hasty Draught" of an Infirmary, which he said was a "challenge" of Pepys' promise to promote the idea. By February, Evelyn had shown his plan to the King, who was "well pleased." Thereupon, Evelyn drew up an elaborate scheme for a hospital for seamen at Greenwich, which, he said, "would save thousands to his Majesty," and sent it to Pepys, whose "dexterity, addresse, and friendship" he hoped would place the proposal before the King. Pepys wrote at once to tell him of his "proceeding towards the advancement of your so laudable design of public infirmaries,"[13] which he put before his fellow officers at the very next meeting. For Pepys was shrewd enough to know by then that Evelyn was a "most worthy person," and that, moreover, his idea for a hospital was a good one. "Mr. Evelyn and I," he reported in his Diary,

rode together with excellent discourse till we came to Clapham, talking of the vanity and vices of the Court, which makes it a most contemptible thing; and indeed in all his discourse I find him a most worthy person. Particularly he entertained me with discourse of an Infirmary, which he hath projected for the sick and wounded seamen against the next year, which I mightily approve of; and will endeavour to promote it, being a worthy thing, and of use, and will save money.[14]

And after a further exchange of letters in which Evelyn assembled detailed information as to the cost of building and of maintenance, Pepys recorded in his Diary, "Mr. Evelyn's proposition about publique Infirmarys was read and agreed on, he being there," [15] but, observed Evelyn in his Diary, "I saw no mony, tho' a very moderate expense would have saved thousands to his Ma^{ty}." [16] Twenty years later, in spite of the support of the Navy Board, Evelyn was still petitioning Parliament to repay him the money he contributed to this building in 1666, and it was not until 1696, when he was an old man, that the corner stone was actually laid, and he made Treasurer.

After the reading and approving of Evelyn's proposal in 1665, Pepys, feeling increasingly genial towards this worthy new acquaintance, invited him home to dinner. "At noon I took him home to dinner, being desirous of keeping my acquaintance with him; and a most excellent humoured man I still find him, and mighty knowing." [17] Pepys was beginning to appreciate this "mighty knowing" quality of Evelyn's, which never failed him in the midst of all their perplexities. Fortunately it proved a less difficult business for Pepys and Evelyn to lay the foundations for a long and rewarding friendship, than to persuade the government to lay the corner stone for a naval hospital.

And so away to Mr. Evelyn's to discourse of our confounded business of prisoners, and sick and wounded seamen, wherein he and we are so much put out of order. And here he showed me his gardens, which are for variety of evergreens, and hedges of holly, the finest things I ever saw in my life. Thence in his coach to Greenwich, and there to my office, all the way having fine discourse of trees and the nature of vegetables.[18]

III

But it was not only the Dutch War and its sufferers which brought Pepys and Evelyn together that unhappy September in 1665. Because of the increase of the plague the Court had removed to Oxford, and both of them had sent their families to the country. "I sent my Wife and whole family . . . to my Brother's at Wotton," wrote Evelyn in his Diary on August 28, "being resolved to stay at my house myselfe, and to looke after my charge, trusting in the providence and goodnesse of God," his "charge" having now extended from the sick and the wounded to include those suffering from the plague. One can see his tall thin figure walking the streets of an empty London. "I went all along the citty and suburbs from Kent Streete to St James's, a dismal passage, and dangerous to see so many coffines expos'd in the streetes, now thin of people; the shops shut up, and all in mournful silence, not knowing whose turn might be next."[19] Pepys, too, was walking through a London where "grass grows all up and down White Hall court, and nobody but poor wretches in the street,"[20] where "every body's looks, and discourse in the street is of death, and nothing else, and few people going up and down."[21] He had sent his wife and her maid Mercer to Woolwich, himself remaining in his lodgings near the Navy Office, until the King insisted that the Navy Board move its offices to Greenwich. Pepys made his will on August 13, "so that," as he piously noted in his Diary, "I shall be in much better state of soul, I hope, if it should please the Lord to call me away this sickly time," and then enjoyed himself with his Valentine. "And there to my Valentine. Round about and next door on every side is the plague, but I did not value it."[22] Moreover, though he was constantly "in fear of the plague," his accounts showed to his content that his "late gettings" had been very great, and that he was "likely to have yet a few more profitable jobbs in a little while."[23] He was able to write at the close of July, "Thus I ended this month with the greatest joy that ever I did any in my life," having enjoyed many "pleasant journies, and brave entertainments, and without cost of money." Pepys kept himself in spirits, in spite of the weekly Bills of Mortality, until he chanced to meet Mr. Evelyn in the street, who told him of "the sad condition at this very day at Deptford for the plague, and more at Deale . . . that the towne is almost quite depopulated."[24]

IV

Though Pepys had a busy, cheerful sojourn in London during the plague and Evelyn a very mournful one, the King, upon his return to Hampton Court in January 1666, thanked them with equal warmth. Charles singled out Pepys at Hampton Court, to express his gratitude to him for his "good service all this year," which sent Pepys to bed "in a great delirium of joy." Evelyn, on the other hand, though the King ran towards him and graciously thanked him for his "care and faithfulnesse in his service in a time of such great danger, when every body fled their employments," sighed, and wrote in his Diary that he did but do his duty, and added, "O that I had perform'd it as I ought." [25]

When, the following September, the Great Fire destroyed the London familiar to Pepys and Evelyn, the King had cause to thank them again for acting as they ought, each in his own way. While Evelyn was having public prayers said at home, Pepys was burying his Parmezan cheese, his naval papers, and his wine in his back yard; while Evelyn, with his wife and son, was meditatively gazing at "that dismal spectacle, the whole city in dreadfull flames neare the waterside," from his coach on the Bankside, Pepys in his nightgown, mounted on a cart sent by Lady Batten, was looking with amazement at the strange sight of London in flames. "And, Lord! to see how the streets and the highways are crowded with people running and riding, and getting of carts at any rate to fetch away things." [26] But Pepys, even before he had rescued his own possessions, hurried off to the King and persuaded him to bring workmen from Deptford to tear down the buildings surrounding the Navy Office, and thus actually preserved it from the fire; Evelyn, on the other hand, was so struck by the astonishing spectacle of ten thousand houses "all in one flame," that he could do nothing but gaze at the "fiery aspect" of the sky, "like the top of a burning oven," casting a light for forty miles around. "The noise and cracking and thunder of the impetuous flames, ye shreiking of women and children, the hurry of people, the fall of towers, houses, and churches, was like an hideous storme," [27] Evelyn walked from Whitehall to London Bridge a few days later "over heaps of burning rubbish," losing himself among the streets he knew so well, and painfully burning the soles of his feet. Only a week before the fire Evelyn had been sent by the King, with Sir Christopher Wren, the Bishop of London, and the Dean of St. Paul's to draw up recommendations for the restoration of St. Paul's. Evelyn and Wren were opposed to rebuilding the steeple: "We had a mind to build it with a noble cupola, a forme of church-building not as yet known in England, but of wonderfull grace." Now Evelyn could consider not only a new St. Paul's but a new London. In his pamphlet addressed to the King in 1661, called *Fumifugium, or The inconvenience of the aer, and smoake of London dissipated,* Evelyn had, "with just Indignation," expressed his dislike of the old London, "That the *Buildings* should be composed of such a Congestion of Misshapen and extravagant Houses; That the *Streetes* should be so narrow and incommodious. . . . That there should be so ill and uneasie a form of *Paving* under foot, so troublesome and malicious a disposure of the *Spouts* and *Gutters* over head."[28] Now the fire had swept away a great part of this medieval city, "full of Stink and Darknesse," and Evelyn immediately drew plans for a modern city which he talked over with the King, the Queen, and the Duke of York. They were "extremely pleased" with his survey, but it was a modified old London and not Evelyn's new city which gradually grew up from the "heaps of smoking rubbish."

Pepys offered a suggestion to the King,—that the buildings around the Navy Office be torn down before the fire reached that part of London, and the Office itself saved from destruction; Evelyn, on the other hand, drew up an elaborate scheme for the rebuilding of all of London after the fire. But Pepys' plan was practical and therefore it was acted upon at once, while Evelyn's, soon found to be visionary, was quietly laid away among his other "projects" and unfinished "designs."

V

During this year of disasters Pepys and Evelyn were constantly meeting, at the booksellers, in the Mall, at the Bell Tavern or in Whitehall. "Good Mr. Evelyn" was usually crying out against the events of the moment. When Pepys met him in Whitehall several weeks after the fire, Evelyn observed "that none of the nobility come out of the country at all to help the King, or comfort him, or prevent commotions at this fire." The King was treated as though he were nobody; there were no priests to comfort the poor people, "but all is dead, nothing of good in any of their minds." Evelyn bemoaned it, and feared that more ruin was to come. Then Pepys hastened away by coach to call for his wife "at Unthanke's," before she should buy a "gown of 15 s. per yard." [29] When they met again Pepys respectfully listened to Evelyn's dark view of the "posture" of the times. "So I to Westminster Hall, and there met my good friend Mr. Evelyn, and walked with him a good while, lamenting our condition for want of good council, and the King's minding of his business and servants." [30] He did not, however, quite succumb to the depression of his older friend. "I out to the Bell Taverne, and thither comes Doll to me," he added immediately after his account of the conversation with Evelyn. But Evelyn's unfailing pessimism, together with his sober gossip about the "young rogues" of the Court, held Pepys enthralled. On April 26, 1667, Pepys took "a turn with Mr. Evelyn," with whom he walked two hours, "till almost one of the clock: talking of the badness of the Government, where nothing but wickedness, and wicked men and women command the King." Pepys reported this conversation in detail in his Diary, sympathizing entirely with Evelyn's displeasure that a Bishop was never seen about the King, that his seventeenth whore, Mrs. Byron, did not leave him until she had "got him to give her an order for £4,000 worth of plate to be made for her," that the servants in the Court lacked bread, having received no wages since the King's return, that the King should squander his revenue by making his bastards princes, and that the Knights of the Garter should wear ceremonial robes "all day till night," and ride in the Park in hackney coaches, "a most scandalous thing, so as all gravity may be said to be lost among us." What more delightful to these two sober citizens than the news that the beautiful Mrs. Stewart had married Lord Richmond to save herself from becoming the King's mistress, and that Sir Thomas Clifford, whom Pepys took for "a very rich and learned man," was a parson's son of little learning, worth only "about seven-score pounds a-year." [31] When Pepys found himself on June 3, 1667, at "a good dinner of plain meat," and good company at the table, it was the "good Mr. Evelyn," with whom, after dinner, he "stepped aside, and talked upon the present posture of our affairs. . . . But, for aught we see, the Kingdom is likely to be lost." [32] Several months later Evelyn's view of the political situation was even darker. He met Pepys on the street and told him that "wise men do prepare to remove abroad what they have, for that we must be ruined," [33] and later Pepys remembered that Mr. Evelyn predicted "we should soon see ourselves fall into a commonwealth again." [34] The dinners during those days were bad; when the meals were over these friends were glad enough to part. Pepys recorded at this time:

And comes to me Mr. Evelyn of Deptford, a worthy good man, and dined with me, but a bad dinner; who is grieved for, and speaks openly to me his thoughts of, the times, and our ruin approaching; and all by the folly of the King. His business to me was about some ground of his, at Deptford, next to the King's yard: and after dinner we parted.[35]

The business of the ground at Deptford was, indeed, settled to Evelyn's satisfaction. He was able to purchase a hundred acres of land to add to the estate of his father-in-law, Sir Richard Browne, whose comfortable manor house of Sayes Court Evelyn had occupied since 1652. There Evelyn, who, during the days of the fighting between the Royalists and the Rebels, had spent his time building a fish pond, an island, and "other solitudes and retirements" at his family seat of Wotton, now laid out one of the famous gardens of his time, visited by the Queen Mother, Lord Chancellor Clarendon, and the Duke of York. Finally Charles himself came to Deptford to honor Evelyn's "poore villa with his presence, viewing the gardens and even every roome of the house, and was pleas'd to take a small refreshment." [36]

Though Evelyn complained so bitterly to Pepys of the King's follies, he was nevertheless one of Charles' most devoted friends, while Pepys always remained only a useful citizen. Evelyn loved Charles, and was able to write of him after his death:

He was a Prince of many virtues, and many greate imperfections; debonaire, easy of accesse, not bloudy nor cruel . . . he lov'd planting and building, and brought in a politer way of living which pass'd to luxury and intolerable expense. . . . He was ever kind to me, and very gracious upon all occasions, and therefore I cannot, without ingratitude, but deplore his losse, which for many respects, as well as duty, I do with all my soul."[37]

Evelyn had refused to be present at the execution of Charles I, and had remained faithful to the Royal Family during the time of the Civil War, though he expressed his loyalty only by sending his "black manège horse and furniture" by a friend to the King then at Oxford, and by pursuing his inquiries into chemistry, painting, languages, and architecture in France and Italy, thus escaping the Covenant Act. He described the funeral of Cromwell as "the joyfullest" he had ever seen, "for there were none that cried but dogs," and he rejoiced when Charles was restored "after a most bloudy and unreasonable rebellion of neare 20 yeares."[38] Though he himself was ill when a company, of which Pepys was a member, set sail for Holland to bring Charles back to England, he occupied his time by writing a laudatory poem to Charles.

> Mistaken Patriots, ignorant and proud
> With furious zeal may bawl in Senate loud.

and so on, for 168 lines, which he presented to his Majesty in "ye Privie Chamber," and had copies made for the Lord Chancellor and several of the noblemen who came to him for it.

Probably Charles had not forgotten Evelyn's translation of François de la Mothe Le Vayer's *Liberty and Servitude* in 1649, on Evelyn's copy of which is written in his hand, "I was like to be called in question by the Rebells for this booke, being published a few days before his Majesty's decollation," nor his famous *Apology for the Royal Party,* published in 1659, "in this time of danger, when it was capital to speake or write in favour of him. It was twice printed, so universaly it took."[39] Certainly Charles looked on Evelyn with especial kindness, when he was again established in Whitehall, and graciously accepted Mrs. Evelyn's miniature of the Madonna copied from a painting after Raphael. He placed the little drawing in his cabinet of treasures and promised to make Mrs. Evelyn lady of the jewels to the future queen, a promise which was quickly forgotten by this urbane King. Evelyn himself was invited to become Knight of the Bath with a group of other gentlemen before the Coronation, but he declined this honor for who knows what obscure reasons of economy or pride.

But it was for his varied learning especially that Charles loved Evelyn. For there were not many in the company of courtiers and fine ladies surrounding the King who could converse with him so knowingly about his collections of miniatures, his ship models, old maps, and medals. And none had such a practised eye as Evelyn, who first discovered Grinling Gibbons working on his carving through the window of a "thatched house, in a field in our parish near Sayes Court." Evelyn brought him to Charles at once; he was so pleased by the piece of carving on which Gibbons was engaged that he had it carried to the Queen, who liked it until the King left the room, and then began to find fault with it, egged on by "a French pedling woman . . . who us'd to bring peticoates and fanns, and baubles out of France to the Ladys." [40] Evelyn carried away the carving "in a kind of indignation," but Charles had seen enough to employ Gibbons for the rest of his life on the carving for St. James, Windsor Chapel at Whitehall, and the new St. Paul's.

Not only was Evelyn's artistic perception beyond reproach, but so also was his sense of the order and decorum which should prevail at Court. When a quarrel arose on the streets of London, a quarrel which resulted in drawn swords and several deaths, waged between the followers of the French and Spanish ambassadors as to which should head the march through London to wait on the King, it was Evelyn who was able to draw up a just account of the incident. He read it to Charles, who immediately ordered one copy to be sent to the ambassador at Paris and another to be published in London. But Charles could not dwell on these unpleasantnesses for too long a time when he might be talking to Evelyn of more interesting matters. "Before I went out of the King's closet, he cal'd me back to shew me some ivorie statues, and other curiosities that I had not seene before." [41]

The learned Evelyn was made Latin Secretary to his Majesty in 1670, "a place of more honour and dignity than profit." [42] Perhaps this position, which enabled him to come and go in Whitehall with perfect freedom, also permitted him to admonish the King in other directions. In any case, he convinced the King of the frivolity and affectation of the elaborate costumes of his courtiers by his *Tyranus or The Mode, or an invective against that unconstancy in our much affecting the French fashion.* In this little pamphlet, Evelyn took occasion "to describe the comelinesse and usefulness of the Persian Clothing." On October 18, 1666, Evelyn tells us, Charles "put himself solemnly into the Eastern fashion of vest . . . resolving never to alter it." Though Charles was not able to do away with the smoke of London which Evelyn complained of in *Fumifugium*, Evelyn's indignation was at least responsible for the lime trees now growing so pleasantly in St. James'. Nor did Evelyn let Charles forget his new interest in the Royal Society, about which he was "pleas'd to discourse" one evening "as he sat at supper in the withdrawing room to his bed-chamber." [43] He showed the King "the perpetual motion sent to me by Dr. Stokes," and talked with him of "a new vernish for the ships instead of pitch." [44]

Though Evelyn very courteously guided the King in matters of dress and gardens, and talked very learnedly to him of bees and painting, clothes and astronomy, glass granados and ivories, he himself was not proof against errors of judgment when he turned his attention to business enterprises. In 1666 John Kiviet, a Dutchman of the Prince of Orange's party, came to the Court with a proposal for embanking the Thames with bricks "both lasting and ornamental," from the Temple to the Tower. He was very soon knighted by the King, and had no trouble in persuading Evelyn to join with him in a great brick-making undertaking, and even to subscribe 50,000 bricks for the building of a college for the Royal Society. After several brief entries in Evelyn's Diary reporting the progress of the venture, we read, on March 26, 1667, "Sir John Kiviet din'd with me. We went to search for brick earth in order to a greate undertaking," and then no more from Evelyn. From Pepys we learn that, on September 23, 1668, "comes Mr. Evelyn to me, about some business with the Office, and there in discourse he tells me of his loss, to the value of £500, which he hath met with, in a late attempt of making of bricks upon an adventure with others, by which he presumed to have got a great deal of money." We are forced to moralize with Pepys, "I see the most ingenious men may sometimes be mistaken."

Pepys, who at this time stood amazed before his mounting savings, could never be so simple as Evelyn in his business judgments; nor could this energetic son of a tailor, who viewed the Coronation from four until eleven from a rafter in Westminster, ever come so near the person of his sovereign as Evelyn. He, indeed, rode to the Coronation in the coach of Lord Mordaunt, and enjoyed to the full the rich embroidery and the jewels, the prancing horses, the flower-strewn streets and the houses hung with tapestry, and even the "speeches made at severall triumphal arches." [45] Perhaps Pepys, who belonged to the Rota or Coffee Club, founded by James Harrington to discuss politics, could never feel quite such veneration for royalty, being more pleased than the aristocratic Evelyn by the observation, which was borne in upon him after a trip down the Thames in Charles' yacht, that kings and dukes are much like other men. While "good Mr. Evelyn" cried out against the gaming tables in Whitehall and the sight of the King talking to the "impudent comedian," Mrs. Nelly, over her garden fence, Pepys, who in his more serious moments shared Evelyn's respectable attitude, glutted himself with looking at the beautiful Castlemaine's shifts, hanging out to dry in the sun.

VI

But more serious apprehensions filled the minds of Pepys and Evelyn at that time than the passing scandals of the Court. War with Holland had broken out again, and now, as Pepys told Evelyn after "a good dinner of plain meat," on June 3, 1667, "the Dutch are known to be abroad with eighty sail of ships of war, and twenty fire-ships; and the French come into the Channell with twenty sail of men-of-war, and five fire-ships, while we have not a ship at sea to do them any hurt with." True, the English ambassadors were parleying at Breda, but the Dutch thought that they were begging peace, and used them accordingly. All this, Pepys believed, was caused by the negligence of the King, who might have controlled the situation. But now it seemed that all was lost. "This discourse of ours ended with sorrowful reflections upon our condition, and so broke up."

Pepys' and Evelyn's conclusion, that "the Kingdom is likely to be lost," was not far wrong. For a week after their conversation, on June 10, 1667, news was brought that the Dutch fleet had entered the Thames "up as far as the Nore." Pepys went at once to Deptford, "and pitched upon ships and set men to work: but, Lord! to see how backwardly things move at this pinch." The seamen, indeed, had been so long without pay that it was impossible to convince them that money had actually been sent to the ships. Pepys took boat to Greenwich, when he heard of the confusion in that town, and found that the Duke of Albemarle had just arrived, "with a great many idle lords and gentlemen, with their pistols and fooleries." The townspeople were removing their goods, Pepys learned over his lunch at the tavern, and had no wish to defend the town against attack. Two days later, on June 12, "newes is come to Court of the Dutch breaking the Chaine at Chatham," which struck Pepys "to the heart." When he heard that the Dutch had burned the English ships, even the *Royal Charles,* Pepys was "so full of this ill news" that he could not write it down. He resolved to consult with his wife and his father as to where to conceal the little money he had at hand, despairing of that which was owed him by the King. All the following afternoon he sat in his office asking news of everybody who came to him. The reports were uncertain, now better, now worse. Some talked of treason, saying that they were bought and sold, that the Papists betrayed them, that those who surrounded the King had given them over to the French. Pepys was not slow to realize that an investigation must soon follow, now that the Dutch were held in check at Chatham with several of their best ships sunk. He spent Sunday working at the office, "to look out" some of his old letters to Sir W. Coventry so as to prepare to justify his Office, and was busy at home all afternoon, though he "did show some dalliance" to his maid, Nell.[46] The next day he set his clerks to work transcribing portions of letters, which he did "collect against a black day to defend the office with"—and himself. On the following Wednesday he was called to attend the Council-board, with all his "books and papers touching the Medway." Though he was certain that the chief blame would fall on Commissioner Pett, he was not able to enjoy his meal before the trial. Nor was he encouraged by his encounter with Evelyn in the lobby of the Council-chamber.

I eat a little bit in haste at Sir W. Batten's, without much comfort, being fearful, though I shew it not, and to my office and get up some papers, and found out the most material letters and orders in our books, and so took coach and to the Council-chamber lobby, where I met Mr. Evelyn, who do miserably decry our follies that bring all this misery upon us.[47]

While Pepys and Evelyn were "discoursing over" their public misfortunes, Pepys was called in to a large Committee of the Council where he told them "to their full content" what his Office had done, and showed them the letters of Sir William Coventry. Pepys at last was allowed to go away with his books and papers, through the crowds of people whom he felt obliged to greet with smiles and salutes lest they should think him a prisoner.

This was only a preliminary investigation, however, for by now the House of Commons was in a storm against the principal officers of the Navy, who, on October 22, 1667, were ordered to defend themselves against the charge of neglecting the defense of the Medway. Though Pepys stayed up until almost two o'clock on October 21, collecting data on all that had been done from the beginning, "touching the safety of the River Medway and Chatham," and "slept but ill all the last part of the night, for fear of this day's success in Parliament," he nevertheless acquitted himself well again. This unexpected success "makes me a little proud," he confessed in his Diary, "but yet not secure but we may yet meet with a back-blow which we see not."

The "back-blow" did not come, for, on March 5, 1668, at the final hearing, Pepys was again the man who, with his thorough knowledge of all the material, was able to defend the Navy Board. A month before the great trial Pepys asked Evelyn to draw him "the prospect of the Medway while the Hollander rode master in it," and Evelyn promptly sent him a pretty pen-and-ink sketch, which is still to be seen among Pepys' naval papers in the Bodleian. He found it difficult to thank Evelyn sufficiently for, he wrote his faithful friend, "the sight of it hath led me to such reflections on my particular interest (by my employment) in the reproach due to that miscarriage, as have given me little less disquiet than he is fancied to have, who found his face in Michael Angelo's Hell."[48]

PUBLICK EMPLOYMENT

The night before the trial Pepys lay "troubling" himself till six o'clock, when he at last woke his wife to comfort him. He comforted himself further with half a pint of mulled sack at the Dog, and a dram of brandy at Mrs. Hewlett's, and was able to speak in Parliament for three hours, he boasted, "most acceptably and smoothly, . . . without any hesitation or losse, but with full scope, and all my reason free about me, as if it had been at my own table." The Navy was completely exonerated. "And so with our hearts mightily overjoyed at this success, we all to dinner at Lord Brouncker's." The following morning Pepys spent "walking in the Hall, being complimented by every body with admiration"; Sir W. Coventry greeted him with, "Good morrow, Mr. Pepys, that must be Speaker of the Parliament-house"; he overtook the King in the Park, who stopped him to say, "Mr. Pepys, I am very glad of your success yesterday." He ended the day pleasantly, with his wife, "talking and playing at cards a little"—Pepys, his wife, W. Hewer, and Deb.

VII

Soon after this triumph Pepys' public and private life underwent a complete change. His eyes failed him, and he closed his Diary forever. He and his wife set out in June on a tour of Holland and France, carrying with them careful directions from Evelyn as to how to enjoy themselves in Paris. Several weeks after their return to London Mrs. Pepys died. Pepys' official life was, if anything, more pressing in the years to follow. In 1672 he was made Elder Brother of Trinity House; in 1673 he became member of the House of Commons, and Secretary to the Office of Lord High Admiral of England. The Test Act led to the resignation of the office of Lord High Admiral by James, Duke of York, and the Admiralty was then placed in Commission. Pepys' untiring energy and genius for organization soon put him in control of the Navy Office, though it was constitutionally under the guidance of the King and the Commissioners. The great concern of the administration at that time was to bring the third Dutch War to a successful conclusion, and then to rebuild the Navy. In 1677, £600,000 was assigned for the building of thirty new ships, and this Pepys, at least, thought was the result of his speech in Parliament on February 23, 1677. Besides rebuilding the Navy, Pepys initiated reforms in the training and discipline of seamen, and took an active part in the inauguration of the King's Mathematical School, as a part of Christ's Hospital, for the training of boys for the King's Navy.*

Despite his admirable work as Secretary, Pepys found himself, together with his friend, Sir Anthony Deane, the famous shipwright, imprisoned in the Tower in 1679, on a charge of selling naval secrets to the French, with the design of overthrowing the government and introducing the Catholic religion. The accusation, which was baseless, was brought against him by a certain John Scott, who later proved to be a notorious international criminal, against whom Pepys had been collecting evidence. The faithful Evelyn dined with Pepys in the Tower on June 4, 1679, and wrote in his Diary, "I believe he was unjustly charged." Evelyn never wavered in his loyalty, in spite of *A Hue and Cry after P. and H.* which appeared in 1679, and Andrew Marvel's *Black Book*, or "A List of the principal labourers in the great design of Popery and arbitrary Power," in which it was said of Pepys that he was once a tailor, and later a serving man to Lord Sandwich, now Secretary to the Admiralty and that he had "got by passes and other illegal wages £40,000."

On his liberation from the Tower, nearly a year later, Pepys found his position as Secretary to the Admiralty occupied by Thomas Hayter, and himself ejected from his official residence at Derby House. He went at this time to live with his friend William Hewer; there he arranged his books and ironically observed the gross mismanagement of the Navy Office by Thomas Hayter and his Commissioners, which was allowed to continue for the next four years.

During these turbulent years in Pepys' public life his connection with Evelyn somewhat lapsed, though there was still an exchange of official communications between Mr. Secretary Pepys and Commissioner Evelyn. We read in Evelyn's Diary of a "mock siege" of Windsor Castle from the Thames given for the King, which he and Pepys both attended. "Being night, it made a formidable shew," said Evelyn, and when the siege was over, "I went with Mr. Pepys back to London, where we arriv'd about 3 in the morning."[49] What

---

* See Rudolf Kirk, *Mr. Pepys upon the State of Christ-Hospital*, Philadelphia, 1935.

they discussed in the coach to London till three in the morning would have been told us in detail by Pepys if his Diary had not come to a close some years before. From Evelyn's entry we can at least conclude that he considered his trip to Windsor with the well-known Mr. Pepys important enough to record in his Diary, in which, before 1669, there was no mention of Pepys at all.

For, though Evelyn enjoyed his "cell" at Sayes Court, and found it difficult to exchange his charming garden for smoky London, he looked upon prominent public characters with vast respect. In 1667 he wrote an eager defense of the "active life" in his answer to George MacKenzie's epicurean view expressed in *Public Employment and an Active Life*. In this little book Evelyn roundly denounced the idler, "sitting on a cushion picking his teeth," and "lying at the feet of his pretty female—sighing and looking babies in her eyes." He himself was drawn somewhat into the active life he so much admired when, in 1671, he was made a member of the important Council of Foreign Plantations. But it was Pepys who had given himself over to "public employment," and left Evelyn musing upon the servility of courtiers who reminded that country gentleman of Horace's city mouse, and moved him to "bless God for [his] private condition." Evelyn had been translating Freart's *Idea of the Perfection of Painting* in his secluded manor house at Deptford; he had been helping his dear friends, Lord and Lady Godolphin, to design the marble fireplaces for their new house on the Thames, near Whitehall; he had been persuading the casual Sir Henry Howard to give the marbles, brought home from Greece by his grandfather, and now strewn over his house and garden in the Strand, to Oxford University.

But now this country mouse wished to be a town mouse again, and he wrote to his old friend Pepys, just out of the Tower, asking him to use his influence towards securing him a place on the Navy Board, where his lack of "profounder Science" might perhaps be remedied by "an extraordinary application & religious integrity."[50] Evelyn had always been genuinely interested in the Navy, and Pepys had considered suggesting his name many years before. In 1666 he recorded in his Diary that he rode in Lord Brouncker's coach talking of several matters, "and then of getting Mr. Evelyn or Sir Robert

Murray into the Navy in the room of Sir Thomas Harvey."[51] But nothing more was said of the matter. In the winter of 1680 Evelyn wrote to Pepys that he was "a Candidate for some such thing in this Shuffling of the Cards." Nor can a man who had "given Hostages to Fortune as I have don . . . be reprov'd by so worthy a Friend, as I esteeme you to be; without whose Counsel and Assistance, I should never hope to Emerge in any Sort." To this offer of Evelyn's "humble Service" in any capacity within his "narrow reach" Pepys responded in his usual direct way by making an appointment with him for the following afternoon. But we never hear of Evelyn, whom Mrs. Pepys called "Sir Politick," emerging into public employment, at least by this avenue.

Evelyn, though it was clear that there was nothing by way of advancement to be had from Pepys, continued to write to him with the same elaborate flattery, behind which was certainly a warm affection. In 1682, when Pepys accompanied the Duke of York to Scotland, he escaped shipwreck only because he had chosen to sail on his own yacht, the *Catherine,* rather than in the yacht of the Duke. But before letters arrived in London to report his safety, the news of the wreck of the *Gloucester* and the loss of many lives put Evelyn into a sad state of distress. Surely it was Sir Politick, who, when he heard of Pepys' safety, wrote to him this fine flourish.

'Tis sadly true there were a greate many poore creatures lost, and some gallant persons with them; but there are others worth hundreds saved, and Mr. Pepys was to me the second of those some, and if I could say more to express my joy for it, you should have it under the hand and from the heart of, Sr, your, etc.[52]

One assumes that the first "of those some" in Evelyn's loyal heart was the Duke himself, and that the rescue of these two "gallant persons" made it not difficult for Evelyn to forget the "poore creatures lost," especially when they gave him a chance to turn a noble compliment.

Pepys' voyage to Tangier with Lord Dartmouth the following year gave a further opportunity for an exchange of compliments between these two gentlemen, teacher and pupil in the game of polite friendship. The occasion of the voyage was anything but glorious. It was simply to destroy the fortification which England, in those early beginnings of empire, found too costly to maintain. But that, indeed, was not Pepys' concern, as he explained to Evelyn, "What our work nevertheless is, I am not sollicitous to learn, nor forward to make griefes at, it being handled by our masters as a secret." All that he was sure of was that the ship was a good one, the leader worthy, and the conversation

. . . as delightfull as companions of the first forme in divinity, law, physick, and the usefullest parts of mathematics can render it . . . with the additionall pleasure of concerts . . . of voices, flutes, and violins; and to fill up all (if any thing can do't where Mr. Evelyn is wanting), good humour, good cheere, some good books.

"But, after all," Pepys finished with a flourish which threatened to trip him in mid-flight,

But, after all, Mr. Evelyn is not here, who alone would have beene all this, and without whom all this would be much lesse than it is, were it not that, leaving him behind, I have something in reserve (and safe) to returne to, wherewith to make up whatever my best enquirys and gatherings from abroad, without his guidance, shall (as I am sure they must) prove defective in.[53]

But Pepys' flights were pedestrian enough compared with those of Evelyn, who answered Pepys' communication immediately. "Methinke I respire againe," he wrote, at God Almighty's late Providence in choosing Pepys for this duty, whatever it might be.

Mithinks when you recount to me all the Circumstances of your Voyage, your noble and choyse Companie; such usefull, as well as delightfull Conversation; You leave us so naked at home, that 'til your returne from *Barbarie*, we are in danger of becoming *Barbarians:* The *Heros* are all Embark'd with my Ld. *Dartmouth* and Mr. *Pepys;* nay they seeme to carry along with them not a Colonie onely, but a Colledge, nay an whole Universitie, all the Sciences, all the Arts, and all the Professors of 'em too: What shall [I] say! You seeme to be in the ship that *Athenaeus* speakes of, was so furnish'd with all that the land afforded, as it more resembled an imperial Citty, than the floating, and artificial fabric of a Carpenter.[54]

Pepys did, indeed, return to England in 1684 as something of a hero. For during his absence the affairs of the Navy under Thomas Hayter and his Commissioners grew only worse, until at last on June 10, 1684, Pepys, on the advice of the Duke of York, was reinstated as Secretary of the Admiralty, an office now formally constituted for the first time. Pepys eagerly resumed his work, and, in 1686, made a fresh experiment in organization by establishing a temporary Special Commission for the Recovery of the Navy.

Evelyn at this time held the most responsible public position of his career, that of one of the three Commissioners for the Privy Seal, proving himself a conscientious Protestant, and an inconvenience to James by refusing to put the royal seal on a Catholic prayer book. Evelyn's position now obliged him to take up his residence in Whitehall, and from his apartment in the palace this Commissioner of the Privy Seal wrote to the Secretary of the Admiralty at York Buildings of the shocking condition of the palace stairs leading down to the Thames. Evelyn reminded Pepys that he had promised to order the watchman, "whose station is at the Dore of his Ma^{tys} Yard, very neere my Stayers" [55] to keep the stairs washed and swept, and pointed out to him that this had not been done.

Evelyn held his high position only two years, for James was then able to introduce a Catholic Lord of the Privy Seal. Evelyn was glad enough to return to the country at this time of growing confusion. "Prudent men were for the old foundations," he had written in his Dairy several years earlier. But now no man knew how much of the foundation of English religion and custom James might destroy. After the coming of William and Mary, Evelyn wrote anxiously to Pepys from the country, "to know if in any sort, I may serve you in this prodigious Revolution." You have many friends, he told him, but none more faithful than myself. "We are here as yet," Evelyn wrote, "(I thank God) unmolested; but this shaking menaces every Corner, and the most philosophic breast cannot but be sensible of the motion." [56]

VIII

Pepys had need of a "philosophical breast," for soon after the establishment of William and Mary on the throne he was ordered to deliver up his naval books to Phineas Bowels, his successor at the Admiralty, and was forced to witness what seemed to him the second collapse of his careful work. Evelyn continued to dine with his old friend and listened with uncritical sympathy to Pepys' complaints.

I din'd with Mr. Pepys, late Secretary to the Admiralty, where that excellent shipwright and seaman (for so he had ben and also a Commiss^r of the Navy) Sr Anth^y Deane. Amongst other discourse, and deploring the sad condition of our navy, as now govern'd by unexperienc'd men since this Revolution, he mention'd what exceeding advantage we of this nation had by being the first who built fregats.[57]

In a letter to Pepys of May 10, 1689, Evelyn had signed himself "in all revolution and vicissitudes whatsoever,

> S^r
> Y^r
> Most faithfully steady, humble, and affectionate Servt (*sans Reserve*)"[58]

For Pepys was again under fire, now that his friend and patron, King James, was no longer in command. The defenders of Thomas Hayter's administration of the Navy Office had claimed that the rapid decay of the thirty new ships built under the Act of 1677 was due to Pepys' "want of care in the choice of their materials, as being built either of East country goods, or doted and decayed English timber."[59] Pepys promptly replied by writing what was called, when it appeared in 1690, by the innocuous title of *Memoires of the Royal Navy*. It was, indeed, a defense of the Special Commission of 1686 against "a strong combination . . . raised for the discrediting of the same," and an attack on the mismanagement of Thomas Hayter, under whose regime the ships fell into decay, discipline relaxed, and public funds were wasted. Pepys read his "Remonstrance" to Evelyn, and wrote to him that he would not take the last step, of publishing, before he had consulted "my oracle (your selfe)."[60] Evelyn recorded the consultation in his Diary on June 10, 1690.

Mr. Pepys read to me his Remonstrance, shewing with what malice and injustice he was suspected with Sr Anth. Deane about the timber of wch the 30 ships were built by a late Act of Parliament, with the exceeding danger wch the fleete would shortly be in, by reason of the tyranny and incompetency of those who now manag'd the Admiralty and affaires of the Navy, of wch he gave an accurate state, and shew'd his greate ability.[61]

Evelyn, perhaps half humorously, sent him a signed and sealed statement in which he said, "I have seene and perused certaine *Memoires relating to the Royal Navy of England for Ten Yeares,*" and added he was "thoroughly convinced of the truth of every period."[62] His letter to Pepys, written the day after the reading of the Remonstrances, was far from humorous, however. "So many and so different passions crowd on my thoughts," he wrote,

that I know not which to give vent to: indignation, pitty, sorrow, contempt, and anger; love, esteeme, admiration, and all that can expresse the most generous resentments of one who cannot but take part in the cause of an injured and worthy person!

Pepys would forever "stand like a rock, and dash in pieces all the effects and efforts of spitefull and implacable men."[63] But later in the same month Pepys, now fifty-seven years of age, was put in the Gatehouse, "on suspicion of being affected to King James."[64]

Pepys was held in the Gatehouse for only five days because of his health, and also because the evidence against him was so slight. Evelyn dined with him immediately before he was sent to prison, and again in his home after his release, and made brief notes in his Diary of these two saddest dinners of the many shared by Pepys and Evelyn. "Din'd with Mr. Pepys, who the next day was sent to the Gate-house,"[65] and "I din'd with Mr. Pepys, now suffer'd to return to his house, on account of indisposition."[66]

Evelyn urged Pepys to vindicate himself completely by finishing his book on the history of the Navy, over which they had been consulting for many years. Should not Pepys now do himself right, Evelyn inquired severely, "by publishing that which all good men who love and honour you cannot but rejoice to see? You owe it to God, your country, and yourself."[67]

For the *Memoires of the Royal Navy* seemed to Evelyn no substitute for the great history of the Navy for which they had been collecting material since the early days of their friendship. Six years later

Evelyn was still writing to Pepys about his *Navalia,* which never appeared, though the manuscript volume in the Pepysian Library at Cambridge and the papers copied in twelve volumes of *Miscellanies* show on what a scale the history was projected.

"I feare to aske what progresse you make towards finishing your noble and most desierable work," wrote Evelyn to him in 1696. "Will you never let us see it 'til perfect according to your scale? . . . Time flies a pace, my Friend. 'Tis evening with us; do not expect perfection on this side of life." [68]

About thirty years of time had flown by Pepys since he had first projected his ambitious scheme for a History of the Navy, beginning with Noah's ark and ending with the Dutch Wars. Such a plan seemed to Pepys to sort "mightily" with his genius, and, he added, "if well done, may recommend me much." By 1665 his new friend, Evelyn, was encouraging Pepys, then Clerk of the Acts, by adding to his growing collection of material. Pepys respectfully called upon Evelyn in his home, where he was shown a ledger of a Treasurer of the Navy, Evelyn's great grandfather, "which I seemed mighty fond of," he innocently noted in his Diary, "and he did present me with it, which I take as a great rarity; and he hopes to find me more, older than it." Evelyn showed him also several letters of the old Lord of Leicester, and a sample of Queen Elizabeth's handwriting. "But, Lord!" remarked Pepys, still new to this game of collecting, "how poorly, methinks, they wrote in those days, and in what plain uncut paper." [69]

The disillusioning experience which Evelyn had in attempting to write a history of the Dutch Wars made him, perhaps, the more anxious that Pepys' undertaking should meet with a better fate. Evelyn told the story in his Diary of his venture into history, which began when, after dinner on June 18, 1670, Lord Arlington hinted to Evelyn that His Majesty still wished him to write a history of the war with Holland, which he had before then declined, to the King's displeasure. He was promised all possible assistance from the Secretary's Office, and felt that he could no longer refuse. Evelyn went to work at once. In August, on an official visit to Whitehall, the King stepped on to a balcony with Evelyn, and expressed his pleasure with what he had heard of his progress, adding that he should make his account a "little keene," since the Hollanders had treated the King "very unhandsomely" in various pictures and books.[70] Evelyn worked valiantly on, though he confided to his friend Joseph Williamson that writing history was "labour for a strong beast." He wrote to his patron, the Lord Treasurer, Sir Thomas Clifford, and told him that what he was writing was only a "vestibule" to the superstructure, "which, if my calculations abuse me not . . . will amount to at least 800 or 1000 pages in folio, notwithstanding all the care I can apply to avoid impertinences." [71]

The "vestibule" appeared in 1674. It was dedicated to the King and bore the title *Navigation and Commerce, their Original and Progress, Containing A succinct Account of Traffick in General; its Benefits and Improvements: of Discoveries, Wars and Conflicts at Sea, from the Original of Navigation to this Day; with special Regard to the English Nation; Their several Voyages and Expeditions, to the Beginning of our late Differences with Holland; in which His Majesties Title to the Dominion of the Sea is Asserted against the Naval and later Pretenders*. It is not difficult to see from the title alone why the Ambassador from Holland should have complained to the King of Evelyn's "preface" to his history of the Dutch Wars. When one actually penetrates Evelyn's "vestibule" to his account of the disagreement with Holland, one finds it tortuous and dark indeed. He attempted to brush aside the history of navies before the deluge. "We shall not adventure to divine, who the hardy person was who first resolv'd to trust himself to a Plank within an inch of Death," [72]—but is was hard for Evelyn to leave behind so enticing a speculation. Not for many pages did he come at last to a reference to the English and the Dutch, and then he wrote with such elegant flourishes that one is puzzled to understand how the Ambassador could have been alarmed by his rhetorical insults. It is "the *English* and the *Hollanders,* who Courting the Good Graces of the same Mistress, the Trade of the World, divide the World between them." But "the small and despicable Rudiments" from which the Dutch emerged, and the long and glorious history of England should indicate that dominion of the seas belongs to England for all time.[73]

Evelyn's interpretation of history was very acceptable to his English readers. Nevertheless, on August 12, the King issued a command that the "little book" should be called in, at this time when the peace with Holland was about to be concluded. A week later Charles told Evelyn that he was "extremely pleas'd" with what he had done, and that, though he must publicly seize the books, he would secretly return them to the bookdealers. Evelyn, however, wrote to Pepys in 1682 that he felt himself to have been unkindly used. "In summe, I had no thankes for what I had don, and have ben accounted since (I suppose) a useless fop, and fit onely to plant coleworts, and I can't bussle, nor yet bend to meane submissions, and this, Sir, is the historie of your historian." [74]

This disappointed historian was glad to send to Pepys, at his request, not only all of his now useless manuscript—"I make no scruple of sending you all my blotted fragments"—but also his thoughts on the difficulties of scholarship, which had been gathering in his mind during these years. "Now as to the compiler's province," he wrote, "'tis not easily to be imagined the sea and ocean of *papers, treaties, declarations, relations, letters* and other pieces, that I have ben faine to saile through, reade over, note, and digest, before I set pen to paper." The fatigue, he admitted, was "unsufferable," and oppressed and confounded him more than it enlightened. "And this, Sir, I dare pronounce you will find, before you have prepared all your *materiam substratam* for the noble and usefull worke you are meditating." A better judgment than his own was requisite, Evelyn concluded, trusting that Pepys possessed this "better judgment," "to elect and dispose the materials that were apt for use." [75]

What a relief to Evelyn to send to Pepys his "trash," which had been accumulating in the library at Sayes Court. "I have sent you already *two large sea-charts,* and now with a *third* I transmit the sheetes I have long since blotted about the late *Dutch-War*." Evelyn then listed the items sent to Pepys at that time. "The print of the battail of *Lepanto*"; "The sculptures of the Trajan's pillar"; "Sir Richard Browne's Dispatches"; "A packet of original letters to the greate Earle of Lycester"; "33 *original letters* to and from greete persons during the late Rebellion in England"; "a rude copy of what I delivered to my Lord Arlington concerning the *Fishery* and duty of the *Flag*"—to mention only a few of the long list of documents which Evelyn contributed to the *materiam substratam* of Pepys'

Navalia.[76] Whether Pepys actually explored this manuscript material we do not know; at least he kept it for more than ten long years. On March 28, 1692, he wrote that it was "Restitution-Week" with him, and that the first act of it should be "the acquitting myself honestly towards you in reference to that treasure of papers which I have had of yours so many years in my hands." It seemed a matter of little importance as to which of these two tireless inquirers, who had resolved to let no corner of their studies remain unsearched, should harbor the growing accumulation of curious data. Though Pepys' judgment was no more able to cope with it at last than Evelyn's, they passed many pleasant evenings turning over their letters and folios. Evelyn wrote in his Diary:

Mr. Pepys, late Secretary to the Admiralty, shew'd me a large folio containing the whole mechanic part and art of building royal ships and men of warr, made by Sr Anth. Deane, being so accurate a piece from the very keele to ye lead block, rigging, gunns, victualling, manning, and even to every individual pin and naile, in a method so astonishing and curious, with the draught, both geometrical and in perspective, and severall sections, that I do not think the world can shew the like. I esteeme this booke as an extraordinary jewell.[77]

Not only did Evelyn overwhelm Pepys by his enthusiasm for all kinds of material, but he also introduced into their discussions a confusing scepticism as to the rightness of the English attitude towards the Dutch, which made it still more difficult to write a history of the British Navy. Since the useless death of Evelyn's friend and Pepys' patron, Lord Sandwich, who, in 1672, threw away his life and several ships to disprove the false suspicion of his courage, Evelyn had observed "the folly of hazarding so brave a fleete, and loosing so many good men, for no provocation but that ye Hollanders exceeded us in industrie, and in all things but envy."[78] "Pray," he asked Pepys in a letter of July 7, 1680, "what have wee Gotten by our Late warr wth ye Hollanders, whome Albemarle did Soe Dispise."[79]

Now that his history of the Dutch Wars had been suppressed he could look back on his *Navigation and Commerce* with detachment and admit to Pepys that it was written "to iustify an unsuccessful (I would I could say a Righteous) quarrell."[80] Lord Treasurer Clifford would not allow him to "moderate" his style "when the difference with Holland was to be the subject." [81] If he were to write the book again he would "temper ye Cement after another manner," and say openly what he had to say on the unfounded pretense of England to dominion on the seas. From which Pepys could only conclude that wise men should always be suspicious of histories, "unlesse where there is demonstraĉon, y^t the Authours had noe interest of their owne to Serve, and were not influenc'd by their Superior or publick cry." [82]

That this official historian of the Dutch Wars should call in question the time-honored belief in the right of making foreign vessels strike their sails to the English flag was unorthodox indeed. Pepys, with the rest of England, had rejoiced when, in the treaty of peace with Holland in 1674, the States-General admitted that to be a right which they had before looked upon as a courtesy, and agreed that whole fleets should strike sails to a single ship bearing the English flag. Evelyn's *Navigation and Commerce* had supported this view without any qualifications. Pepys himself had thought at that time of writing a treatise on the rights of the English flag and presenting it to the Duke of York. To have Evelyn now "speake plaine truth," and to tell him his real thoughts, "betweene friends (and under the rose as they say)," [83] though the doctrine be heterodox to what he himself had published, did not simplify the point of view of a former Secretary of the Admiralty about to turn historian.

These matters must be "exquisitely searched into," said Evelyn, and Pepys, furnished with a "noble library," "and instructed by the greatest experience, joyn'd to an Industry and Capacity (beyond any Mortal Man that I know)," was the one to whom "the Learned and curious world" looked for "that hitherto conceil'd *Arcano Mar,"* written "with the most consumate perfection and advantage." Here was a chance for Pepys to make use of all sides of his knowledge, the historical, mathematical and mechanical, the critical and politer learning, for they all lay "fairely within the Circle of that Mysterie, and within your ample Sphere." [84]

It was not difficult to see why "that Mysterie" remained enclosed in a circle when one contemplates the queries, large and small, which Pepys put before Evelyn, on July 7, 1680, and which Evelyn did not fail to answer, after rummaging his "Slender Collections" at Sayes Court.

Instances of any Nationall Mistakes either new or old, whether at home or abroad, in ye over Valueing their owne Knowledge or Force, or undervalueing those of other Countrys, and may not ye Ill Success of ye Spaniards in 88 bee in some measure Charged uppon a Mistake of this Kind in refference to us, as ours seems to be at this day in that against ye Moores in Barbary?

Instances of any Considerable Inventions or particular peeces of Knowledge, Whether in trade, science, or otherwise, Wherein we may rightly Value our Selves before our Neighbours?

Books of Stratagem, & particularly Navall?

Why should other Nations more Ancient in their Navall actions then Wee, be thought less Inventive & Improv'd then us in the art of Navigation, While they are found soe much to outdo us, in all other arts, viz., Architecture, Painting, etc, and most other parts of humane Knowledge, whether for use or Pleasure

Instances of any Defeats anciently given us at Sea, or Invations made uppon our Land by Forrein^{rs} from the Roman Conquest upwards, to this day and more Especially from ye French.

Who was Genebelli that built ye Block Houses in 88 at Gravesend, and first used ye stratagem about three years before of Fire Boats at ye Siege of Antwerp.

Who was Henry ye 8^{ths} Engin^r in ye Castles he built, & have wee ever had any Considerable Ingen^{rs} of our owne Country.

Queen Elizabeths forbidding King Henry ye 4th of France to build any new Ships, may not actions of his implying ye Contrary be Instanced in, Q[uery], ye records in ye Great Wardrobe L Walsinghams words.

The History of D. Dudley, And of Gabot, And the Fight at Lepanto, The Date and Author of The Old Prologue.

Notable Ingorances of a Nation, Such as the burning of a B^{pp} for asserting ye Antipodes.[85]

Evelyn replied that the queries were of that "Substance" as he were "imodest" to pretend he should at any time "much lesse at present" [86] be able to give Pepys full satisfaction. But he would, nevertheless, "cast a mite" into Pepys' "opulent stock" of information, and forthwith he began. "To the first Enquiry a Volume might be Compiled," he said, though unfortunately the writings of Philo, Romanus, the Rhodian, and others have perished. But even without their help Evelyn was able to write many pages of more or less related material, and then passed to the next question, "Wherein do we exceed other nations?" As examples of the supremacy of England, Pepys must

recon our women, Horses, Dogs, Cocks, Rabits, Artichock, Tinn, Lead, Wool, Black Lead, red marking Stone, Oaker, Oakes, Herrings, Paintings in Miniature, Musitians on ye Viol de Gamba & now of late Joyners, Carvers, Lock Smiths, Engine for Weaving Stockins &c Ribbon, Fullers, earth, Sea & Scotch, Coale, Rings of Bells money, Bowling greens, Taverns, Inns, pinns, & Variety of Religions.[87]

"I have no time to Range them in order," apologized Evelyn at last, "and therefore proceed to Shipping."

After what amounted to a small pamphlet of material in reply to his questions, which would have puzzled a better judgment than Pepys', Evelyn drew in his sails. "But S^r I groe Tedious to you, and will therefore now Contract my Sailes, and Come Nearer home."[88]

Pepys did not for a moment look with doubt upon Evelyn's contributions to his history of the Navy. Though they were, for instance, concerned with the history of colors,[89] or with the martial behavior of dogs,[90] all would somehow find a place in this great work. As Pepys wrote to Dr. Charlette in 1694,

And a just reproach I should think it of me to have one hole found unsearched by me, or knowingly to have failed of rendering myself master of any one written sheet that either pains or price could help me to on that subject.[91]

Evelyn continued to add to the complexity of those curious researches for the rest of Pepys' life. One is not surprised to discover that, except for an interesting exchange of letters between Pepys and Evelyn, and many absorbing conversations, nothing came at last of this expenditure of effort. "Besides what he publish'd of an account of the Navy, as he found it and left it," recorded Evelyn with complete detachment in his Diary after Pepys' death in 1703, "he had for divers yeares under his hand the History of the Navy, or *Navalia* as he call'd it; but how far advanc'd, and what will follow of his, is left, I suppose, to his sister's son."[92] John Jackson, who was also Pepys' adopted son, and heir, had the discretion to leave Pepys' manuscripts undisturbed in his library.

Certainly the importance of these two active citizens of London did not lie in their reading of history; they were perhaps too closely involved with the shaping of events to interpret them. It lay rather in the good sense and courage with which they shared in the changes and disasters of those years of "revolutions and Vicissitudes." Both Evelyn and Pepys showed themselves good men in bad times. Evelyn, by temperament a scholar and a dilettante, nevertheless worked to relieve the sufferers from the Dutch War, and those made destitute by fire and plague. Pepys, though far more self-interested than his learned and ingenuous friend, proved himself, indeed, to be almost a great man in the energy and power with which he built up the English Navy, in spite of overwhelming difficulties.

CHAPTER TWO

Private Enjoyment

I

"BUT Lord! to see how fraile a man I am," wrote Pepys in his Diary on May 18, 1665, "subject to my vanities, that can hardly forbear, though pressed with never so much business, my pursuing of pleasure." Plague, fire, revolution, and war; but also, in the life of a seventeenth-century man of the world, a host of "vanities"—etchings, medals, new musical instruments, chemical experiments, and gardens—which neither Evelyn nor Pepys could forbear. For these noble diners-out were men of learning as well as men of affairs, and were able to spend a very good evening over a game of linguistics the moment their concern for Lord Sandwich and the fleet was relieved. The capture at last in the autumn of 1665 of the great East India ships put Pepys into such a state of joy that he at once hurried to one of his favorite retreats, the home of Captain Cocke. There he found other Commissioners already assembled, Lord Brouncker, Sir W. Doily, Mr. Evelyn, and Sir J. Minnes, "a simple, weak man," but "most excellent pleasant company" nevertheless, and the "best mimick" that ever Pepys saw. There they supped.

The receipt of this newes did put us all into such an extacy of joy, that it inspired into Sir J. Minnes and Mr. Evelyn such a spirit of mirth, that in all my life I never met with so merry a two hours as our company this night was. Among other humours, Mr. Evelyn's repeating of some verses made up of nothing but the various acceptations of *may* and *can,* and doing it so aptly upon occasion of something of that nature, and so fast, did make us all die almost with laughing, and did so stop the mouth of Sir J. Minnes in the middle of all his mirth (and in a thing agreeing with his own manner of genius), that I never saw any man so out-done in all my life; and Sir J. Minnes's mirth too to see himself out-done, was the crown of all our mirth. In this humour we sat till about ten at night, and so my Lord and his mistress home, and we to bed, it being one of the times of my life wherein I was the fullest of true sense of joy.[1]

Perhaps Evelyn's aptness for this game of *may* and *can,* which made his fellow Commissioners "die almost with laughing," came from his work on the Royal Society Committee for the Improvement of the English Language, on which he had the previous December served with Dryden, Waller, Sprat, and others. It was at a meeting of the Royal Society, at any rate, where Evelyn and Pepys loved to "refresh among the philosophers," that we first hear of their encountering each other. Pepys, who had only recently become a member, on February 15, 1665, was sufficiently struck by Evelyn's "very particular account" of the making of several sorts of bread in France, to record the reading of the report in his Diary two weeks later.

Evelyn, who returned from his foreign travels in 1652, interested in everything from hieroglyphics to porcelain, who studied chemistry in Paris, and music in Italy, had been associated with the Royal Society since its first meetings in Gresham College in 1660. Though he had passed his years as a law student in London, "studying little but dancing and fooling more," and described himself, at that time, as "of a raw, vain, uncertain and very unwary inclination," he was, in 1661, a respected member of the Council, when the Royal Society was officially incorporated. For he had, during his seven years on the Continent, industriously learned four languages; he had become friends with "Mr. Hobbes, the famous philosopher of Malmesbury," then living in Paris, and discoursed "of chymical matters" with Sir Kenelm Digby, showing him "a particular way of extracting oyle of sulphur." He had, furthermore, penetrated the most important private collections "of achates, chrystals, onyxes, porcelain, medails, statues, relievos, paintings, taille-douces, and antiques"[2] in Italy and France, and drawn sketches of palaces, cathedrals, and fortifications. Finally, he had returned to Wotton, bearing with him a "rare table of veins and nerves" from Padua, the first ever seen in England, which he presented to the Royal Society in 1668. Fifty years after his travels, Evelyn wrote to his friend Henshaw, with whom he traveled in Italy, that he almost grew young again, recalling "the agreeable toile we tooke among the ruines and antiquitys, to admire the superb buildings, visite the cabinets and curiositys of the virtuosi, the sweete walkes by the banks of the Tiber, the Via Flaminia, the gardens & villas of that glorious citty." [3]

Evelyn, indeed, dreamed all of his life of a sort of settlement of kindred spirits who might, by their way of living, make more permanent these delights of civilization, and thus escape the "fond morigeration to the mistaken customs of the age," which robs men not only of their time, "but extremely of their virtue & best advantages." [4] In 1659 he unfolded his idea to Robert Boyle: in his community, he wrote, life was to be spent in reading and conversation, with bowls and chess, and music once a week, and gardening for exercise. "Is not this the same," he inquired, "that many noble personages did at the confusion of the empire by the barbarous Goths" when they wished to retire from the "impertinences of the world?" [5]

Though Evelyn's plan for a settlement of virtuosi, who should "live profitably and sweetly together," remained a dream, as perhaps he intended it should, the Royal Society, with Lord Brouncker as its President, and Charles II as a member, became to Evelyn very much a reality. It was he who, in his Dedication to his translation of Naudés' *Instructions for Erecting of a Library* in 1661, first called the "Philosophical Society" the "Royal Society," and received for this compliment a vote of thanks from "our philosophic assembly." It was Evelyn, too, who felt that the glory of the Royal Society demanded an ode "from the best of poets upon the noblest argument," and persuaded Cowley to compose it. Evelyn himself designed the frontispiece for Sprat's *History of the Royal Society,* which was executed by Hollar, and he offered to the Society his own motto, so characteristic of this intrepid scholar, "Omnia explorate, meliore retinete." Though Evelyn's motto was not adopted by the Society, the "discourses" which he presented at the meetings show that he himself never forgot that all was to be explored. His philosophical contributions to the meetings ranged from his discourse *Of Earth and Vegetation* (1662) to *Panificium, or the several manners of making bread in France where by general concent the best bread is made*

(1665); from *Sculpture* (1662), part of a projected *General History of all Trades,* which would include "a full view of the several arts of Painting in oyl, in miniature, anealing on glass, enamelling and making marble paper," [6] to *Terra, A Philosophical Discourse of Earth,* which so pleased the Society that it ordered the treatise to be published.

Evelyn's eagerness to "explore all" often prevented him from "retaining the best." He traveled as far to see "ye wonderful engine for weaving silk stockings" as to study an Anglo-Saxon manuscript; he secured for the Royal Society not only Henry Howard's library, but also a Spanish plow sent to him by Lord Sandwich when he was Ambassador to Spain. His admiration for the Royal Society knew no bounds; he would not blush, he declared, to pronounce their Assembly as accomplished as any in the whole world, and that "because it does not consist of a company of *Pedants,* & superficial persons; but of *Gentlemen,* and Refined Spirits that are universally Lern'd, that are *Read, Travell'd, Experienc'd* and *Stout."* [7] That the Royal Society thought as well of Evelyn is shown by the fact that he was elected Secretary in 1672, and that in 1682, and again in 1693, he was asked to stand for President. But on both occasions he had to refuse the honor because of ill health.

II

Evelyn was not able to hold this high office, but Pepys was made President of the Society in 1684, and Evelyn was elected to the Council. Pepys, as he himself tells us, lacked philosophy enough to understand the experiments performed at the meetings, but he took great joy in his "fine discourse" among the philosophers, "so sober and so ingenious." He was fascinated by the "chymical glasses and things" in the laboratory of Charles, "but understood none of them." He made no scientific contribution to the Society, it is true, but he did contribute £50, "to be laid out as the Council should direct," for which Mr. Evelyn, Dr. Lister, and Dr. Gale were appointed to wait upon the President with the thanks of the Society.[8] And he did present a letter written by Evelyn to the meeting of October 28, 1685, describing the remarkable effect of a thunder storm on two of the King's ships in the harbor of Portsmouth.⁹

Moreover, he understood the art of giving philosophic dinners. Long after his term of office expired he continued to entertain the most cherished members of the Royal Society on Saturday evenings, in his handsome apartment at York Buildings. We read in Evelyn's Diary, for instance, of an absorbing evening in December of 1685.

> Dining at Mr. Pepys's, Dr. Slayer shewed us an experiment of a wonderful nature, pouring first a very cold liquor into a glass, and super-fusing on it another, to appearance cold and cleare liquor also; it first produced a white cloud, then boiling, divers corruscations and actual flames of fire mingled with the liquor, which being a little shaken together, fixed divers sunns and starrs of real fire, perfectly globular, on the sides of the glasse, and which there stuck like so many constellations, burning most vehemently, and resembling starrs and heavenly bodies, and that for a long space. It seemed to exhibit a theorie of the eduction of light out of the chaos, and the fixing or gathering of the universal light into luminous bodys. This matter or phosphorus was made out of human blood and urine, elucidating the vital flame or heate in animal bodys. A very noble experiment.¹⁰

Here, at The Admiralty, dining with Secretary Pepys, one was certain to pass an evening such as no virtuoso would willingly forego. One might encounter, for instance, "Capt. Baker, who had been lately on the attempt of the North-west Passage." He held the company enthralled for the evening by his report of the "prodigious depth of ice, blew as a sapphire, and as transparent," and of the thick mists, which finally caused his return.¹¹ On another Saturday night, Captain Dampier, the "famous buccaneer," dined with these gentlemen, and brought with him "a map of his observations of the course of the winds in the South Sea," assuring them that the maps hitherto drawn "were all false as to the Pacific Sea." ¹² Again, before a select number of "particular persons," invited to York Buildings by Mr. Pepys, one might listen to the famous singer, Cipaccio, whose talents were obtained with some difficulty, since he disdained to sing before any but princes. On another occasion, "the rare voice of Mr. Pule," lately come from Italy, delighted the guests with "severall compositions of the late Dr. Purcell."[13] The entertainment at the Admiralty dinner was one evening furnished by the son of Dr. Clench, a child not twelve years old, whose "prodigious maturity of knowledge" dazzled the circle of philosophers. Pepys and Evelyn examined the child, with "promiscuous questions, wch required judgment and discernment to answer so readily and so pertinently."

There was not any thing in chronology, history, geography, the several systems of astronomy, courses of the stars, longitude, latitude, doctrine of the spheres, courses and sources of rivers, creeks, harbours, eminent cities, bounderies and bearings of countries, not only in Europe but in any other part of the earth, wch he did not readily resolve and demonstrate his knowledge of, readily drawing out with a pen anything he would describe.[14]

Nor did the examination stop here. Greek and Roman history, the stories of the Old and New Testament, the beliefs of the Gnostics, Sabellians, Arians, and Nestorians, natural and moral philosophy, even metaphysics, were plumbed in the course of the evening until Pepys and Evelyn were themselves exhausted "rather than this wonderfull child, or angel rather, for he was as beautifull and lovely in countenance as in knowledge."

Thus passed the enchanted evenings of these happy possessors of "all the Sciences, all the Arts," whose restless curiosity left nothing unsearched into. When Evelyn was an old man of eighty-three, and Pepys had only a few months more to live, it was these evenings that Evelyn recalled in the last letter to Pepys which we possess. "In the meane time, I feede on the past conversation I once had in York Buildings, and sterve since my friend have forsaken it."[15]

What, one wonders, did they come to think of one another after all of these quaint explorations into art and learning? Evelyn, it is clear, thought of Pepys during the forty years of their friendship in much the same terms as he did when he recorded his death in his Diary in 1703. Pepys was to Evelyn "a worthy, industrious and curious person," whose public position he respected, and whose excursions into the world of virtuosi he thoroughly enjoyed. On one occasion in his Diary Evelyn linked Pepys' name with that of "Mr. Surveyor Dr. Chr. Wren," calling them "two extraordinary ingenious and knowing persons." [16] He dined them both at his home, then carried them off to see the carvings of his new protégé, Grinling Gibbons. In a letter to Pepys in 1692, Evelyn, with characteristic ardor and simplicity, showed with what entire approval he looked upon his friend. *"O Fortunate Mr. Pepys!* who knows, possesses, and injoyes all that's worth the seeking after. Let me live among your inclinations and I shall be happy." [17]

Pepys could hardly have wished to live exclusively among Evelyn's "inclinations"—Evelyn, who as a young man had his portrait painted by Nanteuil, with "Repentance is the beginning of philosophy" inscribed in Greek beneath it. But it is clear that the laborious Evelyn, with his beehives under glass, and his elaborate system of cataloging his books, who not only studied engraving, but also invented an hourglass "for the measure of time at sea," held a peculiar fascination for the more shrewd but less learned Pepys. "And so by water to Deptford," we read many times in Pepys' Diary. Mr. Evelyn "and I walked together in the garden with mighty pleasure, he being a very ingenious man; and the more I know him the more I love him." [18] Pepys, ambitious man of the world though he was, did not fail to appreciate the pleasure of associating with a scholar whose ample private fortune enabled him to travel widely, perfect his collections, and pursue his devious researches in spite of political unrest; whose aristocratic dignity of bearing and genuine hospitality of mind put him on terms of intimacy with all the eminent men of his time, with the King and the Lord Chancellor, with Dryden and Jeremy Taylor.

III

It was to the experienced traveler, Evelyn, that Pepys turned for assistance when he and his wife made their trip through Holland and France in 1669. Nor did he appeal in vain. Evelyn, who had spent many years of his youth roaming about Europe, knew that to dance, to ride horseback, to study languages, and to wear handsome clothes, were "the very shells of travel"; that "the fruit of travel" was to be plucked only by the experienced observer who studied "men, customs, courts, and disciplines, and whatsoever superior excellences the places afford, befitting a person of birth and noble impressions." Such a *grand tour* "sets the crown upon his perfections" when he at last returns "with religion, courage, knowledge and modesty," "the glory of his family, the star and ornament of his age."[19] Nothing could have been more pleasant to Evelyn than to write out in detail for his younger and quite untraveled friend, Pepys, careful instructions for his trip to the Continent.

"I send you my Rhapsodies," wrote Evelyn on the night of August 21, 1669, in response to Pepys' request for suggestions about his journey; they are but "snatches and night-work, and unconnected, which you must pardon, and if you judge it worthy it, cause to be transcrib'd."[20] "The ordinary commerce and import of [the] wild pererations" of most travelers are "the vanity of talk, feather and ribbon"; Pepys must be a more serious traveler, admonished Evelyn. He must make collections of what he found to be excellent, draw plans of palaces, churches, and gardens. "They will greatly refresh you in your Study, and by the fire side, when you are many years return'd."[21] Pepys did cause these lengthy "Rhapsodies" to be transcribed; furthermore he had them handsomely bound, and preserved an engraving of Evelyn and one of himself as a frontispiece to the book.[22] After his return to London in September, Pepys thanked Evelyn briefly as "he to whom singly I owe the much greater part of the satisfaction I have met with in my late voyage,"[23] but he told Evelyn nothing of curious collections, famous antiquities, or noble experiments which he investigated in Paris. He was more interested, indeed, in collecting models of ships and other "navalia" than in sketching monuments. He did, however, carefully put away in his library Evelyn's small guidebook to Paris, and there it may be seen today.

One can imagine Evelyn, as he mapped out a journey for Pepys and his wife through the little French towns between Calais and Paris,[24] recalling the many times he had made that same uncomfortable trip, sometimes with a train of coaches guarded by armed menservants, sometimes on horseback alone. Pepys must halt in his journey occasionally, Evelyn told him, to visit various gardens, waterworks, fortresses, and altars. But he will get little satisfaction from this part of his trip, for it is "a Frontier and miserable country," where one plainly sees the effect of a tyrannical government and continual warfare. Paris, however, will quickly eradicate the impression left by these "miserable places," especially after Pepys has comfortably installed himself and his wife in a "chambre garnie," and made connections with the Irish Doctor of Physick recommended by Sr Saml Tukes, who will be to Pepys "honest, humble & necessary."

A delightful picture of the Paris of the late seventeenth century emerges in one's mind as one reads these entirely practical directions that Evelyn wrote to Pepys. The first thing to do, he told him, after Pepys has rested a little, is to mount the steeple of St. Jacques, "to take a Synoptical Prospect of that monstrous City, to consider ye Situation, Extent, & Approaches; so as to be ye better able to make Comparisons with our London." Descending from the steeple, Pepys must go at once to the Hospital of La Charité, to observe how charity in Paris is dispensed "in so full, so cleanly & devout a manner." This duty over, Pepys is then free to introduce himself to the Duke of Orleans, the most knowing and "curious" person in Europe for medals, who lives in the Luxembourg Palace. "Consider ye Building well, and ye Extent of ye Ground about it, as within so great a City; the Fountains, Walks, Eminency on wch it stands." Then cross the river and enter the Louvre, the court of the Great Monarch. Kiss the King's hand, and the Queen's also; listen to a public audience if that is possible; watch the King and Queen at table, and observe his guard and council, taking note the while of the paintings, furniture, gardens, and "ten thousand Particulars" which will strike your attention. If "ye Giant at ye Entry do not forbid you," enter Notre Dame and notice how inferior it is to St. Paul's and Westminster Abbey.

After these initial curiosities are satisfied, there are still many more excursions to make—to the "Fryers & other Religious Men" (perhaps Evelyn had Cluny in mind), to the Universities, the "melancholy Situation" of which, within the court "has some what (methinks) of particular in it, which affects me." Listen to some public scholastic exercise if you can, "and love our owne Universities ye better after it." Go then to the Law Courts, not far distant, and notice how the lawyers dress, and how they proclaim; seek out, also, a riding academy "to see ye Gent. ride ye Great Horse."

The private collections of books, pictures, statues, and curiosities in the hands of noblemen are too numerous to list, and yet they must be seen, Evelyn insisted. He enclosed three letters of introduction to friends of his in Paris, "though of ye lower Rank," who might help Pepys in this pursuit. At least Pepys will be able to discover from these gentlemen whether Louis Quatorze has done anything for "ye Virtuosi (our Emulators) in designing them a Mathematical College," and, if he has, "seek after it," urged Evelyn, "& procure to be admitted into their present Assembly, that you may render our Society an account of their Proceeding." If Pepys were planning a whole year in Paris, instead of several months, Evelyn would insist on his pursuing a "Course of Chimistry," which is shown "to ye Curious to their wonderful satisfaction and Benefit of Philosophic Spirits."

But on a short visit one can at least see the Bastille, the Gobelins, the public Comedies at L'Hotel de Bourgoyne, "and even ye Mad men at ye Petites-Maisons," "for all of these Places and Humours are instructive." Indeed, Pepys must not neglect to pause many times on the Pont Neuf to contemplate "the Mountebanks and prodigious Concours of Mankind . . . as a lively Image of that Mercurial Nation."

Having inquired sufficiently into the manners of the town, Pepys must "make a Journey about ye Town, to see how they live in ye Country, & how they make their Wine . . . among their Villa's," and, while in the country, he must "take a thorough Survey of their renowned Fountainebleau; which when you have seen you will not judge comparable to Hampton-Court. . . . Yet here ye Canal, & plenty of Water, with ye Forest about it is stupendious." Finally, have your Lady's and your own pictures engraved by Nanteuil. You would then bring home "jewels" to be enjoyed forever. With this suggestion, Evelyn drew his long letter to an abrupt end, "S^r, Had I anything more to add, I should weary you; it is already late & I almost blind."

In a brief note which Evelyn enclosed with his letter he told Pepys that he expected to be paid for his trouble "with fresh and more material Observations" after Pepys had "traversed" the town of Paris.

But those fresh observations were neither recorded by Pepys in his Diary, nor written in letters to Evelyn, for Pepys' Diary was closed the previous May, and now, back again in London, he was afflicted by the sickness of his wife, who, from the first day of her return to London, "hath layn under a fever so severe as at this hour to render her recoverie desperate." [25] Mrs. Pepys did not recover from the fever, and all that we have left of the trip to the continent is several letters of condolence, now in the Bodleian Library, written to Pepys from Paris by the friends they made there during this last trip.

How many of Evelyn's suggestions Pepys followed we shall probably never know; as far as we can discover, however, he did not have his and Mrs. Pepys' pictures done by Nanteuil. Perhaps the best expression we have of Pepys' sense of the importance of his travels is the fact that he financed the *grand tour* of his nephew, John Jackson, which lasted two years (1699–1701), and extended over France, Italy, Spain, and Portugal. Soon after the return of John Jackson, the aged Evelyn wrote to Pepys for advice as to whether or not to establish his grandson, John Evelyn, just up from Oxford, in the Temple. Pepys wrote a long letter to Evelyn in reply, advising him to send his grandson abroad for four or five months before turning him into a lawyer. Evelyn's "young-man" should make such a tour through Holland and Flanders to Paris as Pepys himself made, he said, "by the aid of your instructions . . . to a degree of satisfaction and solid usefulnesse that has stuck by mee through the whole course of my life and business since." This trip, over thirty years ago, taught him to notice the great difference between those "whose knowledge has been widened and refined by travel and others whose observations have been stinted to the narrow practice of their own country." Surely Evelyn has by this time noticed the deference paid to himself "from all the politer world on the account of the distinguishing perfections eminently raised in you from your forreign education in addition to your native." [26] Though Pepys' comment on his trip to Holland and France was delayed some thirty years it must have been gratifying to his guide, who prided himself on his knowledge of the cabinets and curiosities of Europe, to hear at last this sincere acknowledgment of his "distinguishing perfection."

IV

If Pepys, with the rest of "the politer world," deferred to Evelyn's superior knowledge in all matters of interest to the virtuosi, he was not so deferential to Evelyn's creative efforts. Evelyn frequently appealed to Pepys as a critic. "If you dine at home and are free from company," he wrote in 1686, "I will stay a few minutes with you, and present a Poëme, before I embark homeward. Deal like a philosopher and friend with me." [27]

Pepys probably dealt with Evelyn more like a friend than a philosopher. For it was many years before then that Pepys had noticed that Evelyn's numerous books on engraving, numismatics, education, or architecture were not so acceptable to him as Evelyn's conversation. To be sure they were "very pretty,"—"up and fell to reading of Mr. Evelyn's book about Paynting, which is a very pretty book." [28] But they were apt to be somewhat lacking in "matter,"— "I away to my boat . . . reading of Mr. Evelyn's late new book against Solitude, in which I do not find much excess of good matter, though it be pretty for a bye discourse." And sometimes they were plainly above Pepys' head.

I abroad to the office and thence to the Duke of Albemarle, all my way reading a book of Mr. Evelyn's translating and sending me as a present, about directions for gathering a Library; but the book is above my reach.[29]

Evelyn's mind was, after all, more "curious" and "ingenious" than creative. Though he and Waller traveled together in Italy, and though Cowley, Dryden, Denham, and Rochester all enjoyed their exchanges of visits with Evelyn, neither in his Diary nor in his letters do we find discerning remarks about the poetry of any one of these men. Evelyn referred to Milton only once in his Diary, and then as "that Milton who wrote for the Regicides"; after an evening spent hearing Dryden read his poetry, Evelyn observed only that he dined with Mr. Edward Sheldon, where also was Dryden, who said that he was interested in his translation of Virgil and planned to write no more plays. "He read us his prologue and epilogue to his valedictory play now shortly to be acted." [30] The plays of the Court by

Buckingham, Etheridge, Congreve, and others, which proved a daily temptation to Pepys, were easily dismissed by Evelyn. After an evening passed at the theater, he wrote in his Diary, "I did not approve of any such pastime in a time of such judgments and calamities." [31] After seeing a performance of *Hamlet,* Evelyn concluded that "now the old plays began to disgust this refined age, since his Majestie's being so long abroad." [32]

But Evelyn was not sceptical of his own literary power. In his *Memoires for my grand-son,* he listed his tragi-comedy, *Thyrsander,* and a number of poems among the manuscripts carefully preserved with his papers at Wotton. Pepys himself was not without literary ambition, and had already written a romance, *Love a Cheat,* while still at Cambridge. But he had had the discernment to destroy the manuscript. The songs he composed for his flute, such as *Gaze not on Swans* and *Beauty Retire,* were Pepys' evening amusements. Evelyn, one fears, took his writing with a seriousness which was at times a trial to Pepys' more robust temperament. The postscript to Evelyn's letter to Pepys, of March 1, 1688, could hardly have been a source of pleasure to Pepys: "I send you another rag of paper, as the Countryman offerd an handfull of Water to the Persian Monarch; and your Acceptance of such trifles shall be to me a Kingdome." [33] Though Pepys was thoroughly interested in all that he could learn and observe on a visit to Deptford, he had always the fear that Evelyn might read him some of his poetry.

Thence I to the Swan, thinking to have seen Sarah but she was at church, and so I by water to Deptford, and there made a visit to Mr. Evelyn, who, among other things, showed me most excellent painting in little; in distemper, Indian incke, water colours: graveing; and, above all, the whole secret of mezzo-tinto, and the manner of it, which is very pretty, and good things done with it. He read to me very much also of his discourse, he hath been many years and now is about, about Guardenage; which will be a most noble and pleasant piece. He read me part of a play or two of his making, very good, but not as he conceits them, I think, to be. He showed me his Hortus Hyemalis; leaves laid up in a book of several plants kept dry, which preserve colour, however, and look very finely, better than any Herball. In fine, a most excellent person he is, and must be allowed a little for a little conceitedness; but he may well be so, being a man so much above others. He read me, though with too much gusto, some little poems of his own, that were not transcendent, yet one or two very pretty epigrams.

What a relief to read at last, "Here comes in, in the middle of our discourse Captain Cocke, as drunk as a dogg, but could stand, and talk and laugh." [34]

V

Pepys was willing to allow Evelyn "a little for a little conceitedness," for he was a man "so much above others" in learning and taste. One might well wonder whether Pepys really knew how much above his other associates in "learning and taste" Evelyn was. Not only had Evelyn pored over the libraries and collections of Europe, but, with the help of his secretary, Richard Hoare, "an incomparable writer of several hands," Evelyn had been occupied with the assembling, the binding, and the cataloguing of his own library since his trips to the continent as a young man. With Naudés' *Instructions for Erecting of a Library* as a guide, he had carefully arranged his books under the names of Greek gods, Roman Emperiors, plants, the seven sages, the muses, and the graces.

Evelyn had, moreover, studied the famous libraries of England, and had become friends with many of their owners. "Went to visit Sir John Cotton," he wrote in his Diary on March 12, 1668, "who had me into his library, full of good MSS. Greek and Latin, but most famous for those of the Saxon and English Antiquities, collected by his grandfather." And again, "Went to see Mr. Elias Ashmole's Library and curiosities at Lambeth," who showed him "a toad included in amber," as well as his astrological library.[35] He knew very well the King's private library at Whitehall, and was allowed to spend afternoons there, at his "full ease." After dining with the Archbishop at Lambeth in 1687, he "retir'd into the library," which was "exceedingly improv'd"; "there are also divers rare manuscripts in a roome apart."[36] When Dr. Tenison, preacher at St. Martin's Church, conceived the idea, in 1684, of erecting in his parish the first public library, it was John Evelyn and Christopher Wren whom he consulted "about the placeing and structure thereof." Evelyn was impressed by the good Doctor's "laudable designe" of providing books for "young gentlemen or chaplains to noblemen," who otherwise frequented the taverns and coffee houses, and considered it "indeede a greate reproch . . . that so greate a Citty as London should not have a publiq library becoming it. There ought to be one at St Paules: the west end of that church (if ever finish'd) would be a convenient place." [37]

Though Pepys was too much occupied with the affairs of the Navy or with drinking buttered ale at the Swan to follow Evelyn in his excursions through the libraries of England, he nevertheless sufficiently appreciated the learning of his friend to persuade Evelyn to let him include his portrait among those of the eminent men, "illustrious for their parts and erudition," with which he wished to decorate the walls of his library. Evelyn's insistence that his "shallow head" should not be included "amongst those heroes"—"in God's name should a planter of colewort" be among the worthies? [38] —finally wore away, and he was pleased to succumb to Pepys' request. He recorded the important event in his Diary on July 8, 1689, in the following brief terms.

I sat for my picture to Mr. Kneller, for Mr. Pepys, late Secretary to the Admiralty, holding my "Sylva" in my right hand. It was on his long and earnest request, and is plac'd in his Library. Kneller never painted in a more masterly manner.

When Evelyn saw his portrait hanging among the illustrious in Pepys' library his modesty was still further shocked, "for in good earnest," he wrote on August 12, 1689, "when I seriously consider how unfit I am to appear in the classe of those learned gentlemen, I am perfectly asham'd." [39] But he immediately proceeded to justify his inclusion by writing to Pepys a long letter, in which he not only instructed Pepys as to how to improve his various collections, but also said all that had accumulated in his mind in the solitudes of Deptford on the subject of paintings, coins, collections of manuscripts, Academies, and the English language. A copy of this letter written in the careful hand of one of Pepys' scribes is still to be seen among his cherished manuscripts in the Pepysian Library. Whether Pepys preserved the letter because he valued it so highly or because he never found time to read it, one may well wonder.

Though Evelyn wasted some space with his elaborately phrased objections to Pepys' inclusion of his unworthy "head" in his assembly of notables—"Tis pitty and a diminution, so elegant a place & precious collection should have anything in it of vulgar"—the letter is an interesting and important comment on the state of libraries and collections at the end of the seventeenth century. Evelyn, for all his misdirected enthusiasms, was one of the first to perceive the necessity of preserving the treasures of civilization for the public, which, except for the small fortunate group associated with the universities and the Court, had, at that time in England, little access to books, pictures, and statues. Evelyn, who rescued the Arundel Marbles for Oxford, and the Arundel Library for the Royal Society, was concerned with the problem of how to make important private collections of all sorts secure for the people of his time and after. It was a source of pain to him that "so many excellent pieces come after a while to be dispers'd amongst brokers & upholsters, who expose them to the streetes in every dirty and infamous corner." Unworthy heirs scatter rare medals and coins among their "panders and misses," or give them to children "to play at counter with."

Pepys must do his part to rescue these collections from dissolution, for "men curious of books & antiquities have ever had medals in such estimation, & rendered them a most necessary furniture to their libraries." It is best for Pepys to purchase whole collections. "But otherwise, they are likliest met withall amongst the goldsmiths, & casually as one walkes the streetes on foot, & passes by the stalls."

Pepys' idea of collecting portraits of important men of his own time is an excellent one, thought Evelyn. The Earl of Clarendon's father planned "to furnish all the roomes of state and other apartments with the pictures of the most illustrious of our nation," among which he included, as "most agreable to his Ld^s general humor, old Chaucer, Shakspere, Beaumont & Fletcher, who were both in one piece, Spencer, Mr. Waller, Cowley, Hudibras." Evelyn sent the Earl a list of names to "compleate & encourage this noble and singular collection," a long list including such names as Cranmer, "old Latimer," "Ven: Bede," "Sr Thos. Bodley," and many more. But sadly enough, "after all this apparatus and grandeure," the old Earl "died an exile, & in the displeasure of his Majesty & others who envied his rise & fortune." "The buffoons, parasites, pimps, & concubines," who took his place at court, came to nothing either, with their "open & avowed luxurie & profaneness . . . *à la mode de France.*" It was to the Earl of Clarendon that Evelyn dedicated his translation of Naudé's *Instruction for Erecting of a Library,* in 1661, because he was "a greate lover at least of books, & furnish'd a very ample library, writ himselfe an elegant style, favour'd & promoted the designe of the Royal Society," and also was "very kind to me both abroad & at home."

"And so I have don with my Ld Chancelor. But not so soone with my worthy friend Mr Pepys," who nourishes a "learned & laudable curiosity of still improving his choice collection." Do not attempt to get all of your paintings in oil, Evelyn advised, it is too expensive. If you can procure "heads" among the print-sellers in *taille-douce* "I should not reprove it." You will be "exceedingly pleas'd to contemplate the effigies of those who have made such a noise & bustle in the world," either by their "wit & learning," or by their "madness & folly." "Nor would I yet confine you to stop here," added the tireless Evelyn, "but to be continualy gathering as you happen to meet wth other instructive types." Possible collections which Pepys might consider are "batails, sieges, triumphs, justes & tournaments, coronations, cavalcads, & entries of ambassadors, processions, funeral & other pomps, tombs, tryals & executions"—to mention only a few of the "types" on Evelyn's long list. Thus your library might be made in time "suitable to your generous mind & steady virtue."

And it is important in this age which has witnessed so many "sad dispersions" of "noble libraries & cabinets," that men should make such collections. For certainly we in England are peculiarly "defective of good libraries among the gentlemen & in our greatest townes." "This greate & august citty of London," peopled with so many witty and scholarly persons, has hardly one library equipped and endowed for the public. Sir John Cotton, who inherited his library from his noble uncle, does not wish to be disturbed by readers. The libraries of Westminster and Sion College are not "much considerable." Nor are those of Gresham College and the Middle Temple any better. There is some hope that that at St. James may be restored, but Jews and chapmen have purchased and transported many books, together with a cabinet of 10,000 medals, collected by "that hopeful cherisher of greate and noble things Prince Henry." "Were not this losse enough to break a lover's heart?" Where are our Suissets, Bodleys, Lauds, Sheldons, bishops and "opulent chancellors" that they do not improve the collections at Trinity College, Cambridge, at Magdalen College, Christ Church, and Balliol? The library at Lambeth "ebbs & flows like the Thames running by it, at every prelat's succession."

The Bishop of Ely, Dr. Stillingfleete, Dr. Tenison, and Sir Edward Coke all have well-stored libraries, as also has Sir Henry Saville, Mr. Hales of Eton, and Dr. Cosin, late Bishop of Durham. But why is not some "provision made by a publiq law & contribution in every county of England" to build repositories for these books that they may at least be accessible to the clergy? As it is, many of the best libraries are scattered at auction. Sir Kenelm Digby's library, though it was "of more pomp than intrinsic value, as chiefly consisting of modern poets, romances, chymical & astrological bookes," was recently sold in Paris. The Duke of Lauderdaile's library is about to be sold; those of Lord Mailland, the Earl of Anglesey, and several others have already "pass'd under the speare." Isaac Vossius brought many manuscripts from Queen Christina of Sweden. "But those birds have taken their flight & are gone."

"And now I have in good earnest don with libraries; but yet not quite with Mr. Pepys." For, said Evelyn, I would not leave you with the impression that every gentleman's house should be furnished with a notable library. But why should there not be built at the west end of St. Paul's "a stately portico," where the reader might find "a copy of every booke printed within the Citty & Universities." Such a national repository should be supported by "every company and corporation of the Citty, every apprentise at his freedom, assisted at first by a general collection thro-out the nation." But perhaps such a miracle cannot be expected until "kings are philosophers, or philosophers kings; which I think may happen not in this but in Plato's revolution," sighed Evelyn, not being able to look ahead to the great Museum founded a half a century after his death.

The real advantage of libraries being also in the homes of private gentlemen, continued Evelyn, still not wishing to leave the subject of libraries, is that one of them might open a room "where there are chaires & a table," to an Academy for the "art and Improvement of speaking & writing well," such as that set up in Paris by "the late greate Cardinal de Richelieu for the polishing & inriching of the language." Here gentlemen "of the first qualitie" might consider it an honour to read their "ingenious exercises" to "so many civil & polish'd wits." How "usefully entertaining" would such afternoons be where one might hear "essays, poems, translations, & other oratorious productions upon a thousand curious subjects," and where one might enter into conversation, "the most humane & obliging in the world," with "greate dukes & blewe ribbons, ambassadors as well as bishops, abbots, presidents, and other learned men & travellers." Such an Academy would make us ashamed to borrow from the French, and would "inflame, inspire, & kindle another genius and tone of writing, with nervous, natural strength and beauty, genuine and of our owne growth." Such a plan was once designed by "Mr. Cowley, Dr. Sprat, Mr. Waller, the D. of Buckingham, Matt. Clifford, Mr. Dryden, & some other promoters of it." Several meetings were held at Grays Inn, but the death of Cowley, the inconvenience of the place of meeting, the plague, and other troubles intervened, and "it crumbled away & came to nothing." Evelyn himself, "an inferior labourer" on that "intended pyramid," had drawn a plan for "the polishing of the English tongue," which he would send to Pepys if he could "suffer my impertinences."

"And now for shame have don! Methinks I heare you cry out, 'What a ramble has Mr. Evelyn made! what a deale of ground for so little game!'" But indeed Mr. Evelyn was worth following on his ramble. With perhaps pardonable exaggeration Pepys replied that he could "hardly find time to take breath" until he had read through his packet of information, "yet I won't promise to have done reading it this month." He added that he would not ask pardon for not doing what he ought to do, when what he ought was what he could not—that is, write Evelyn a fitting reply to this formidable outpouring of learning. "And yet some answer you shall (in time) have to it, and ye best I can give you, namely, by me endeavouring to leave no one syllable unpractis'd of what you have the goodnesse to teach me in it, and lyes within ye reach of my pate and purse to execute." [40]

VI

When one visits the Pepysian Library at Cambridge, and examines the well-arranged collections of prints and drawings of London, broadside ballads, "heads" of famous men, news pamphlets, not to mention Pepys' library of about three thousand volumes now carefully preserved in precisely the manner he specified, one wonders whether he did not, after all, give a very good answer at last to the letter of his elderly adviser and fellow connoisseur.

Pepys was, indeed, born with the tastes of a collector. In 1660, while at The Hague, he bought three books "for the love of the binding." In 1665 he began seriously to systematize his library, by ordering new bindings for a great many of his old books, thus making his "whole study of the same binding within very few." The next year he and Simpson, the joiner, went to a good deal of trouble to build presses for his books, which were now growing very numerous. He had his binder gild the books all alike, and number each with a paper label. He and his brother John worked over the cataloguing of this library, which kept on growing, in spite of Pepys' vows to buy no more books or prints. Evelyn's admonition to him in 1669 before he left for France—"Pray forget not to visit the Taille-Douce shops, and make Collections of what they have excellent" —need hardly have been made, so eager was Pepys to add to his collections. When his nephew, John Jackson, set out on his *grand tour* in 1699, he carried with him a commission from his uncle not only to purchase for him rare and interesting books, but also a few prints, but those very good, of "publike prosesions, cavalcads, canonizations, or any other solemnitys extraordinery relateing to the Church, anticuteys, or town of Rome." [41] He wanted, he specified to his nephew, "religious prints, and in particular of habits, in your passage through Spain and Portugal, where I fancy the biggotry of those nations may lead them to abound therein." [42] But above all he wished a print of a bullfight, an item not included in Evelyn's list of desirable "types."

Naudés' advice to Evelyn, which he passed on to Pepys, "to rummage and often to revisit the shops of frippery booksellers," led both of these ardent collectors up many a side street of learning. Pepys was constantly writing to Evelyn of his excursions to the book dealers, the auction rooms and print shops. Pepys was out when Evelyn called to see him one evening, and wrote to him the next day, "I was gone but to Covent Garden by chaire, to try whether I could have layd out a little mony well at an auction of prints, upon the enclosed list thereof, but fayled; there coming no heads in play dureing my stay, which was not above ½ an houre." Pepys, still troubled with the stone, in spite of the operation of 1658, and with the gout besides, assured Evelyn that he had not been out of his house for full fourteen days, except to dine last week with Mr. Houblon. "He and I dranke your health and earnestly wished you there, as believing the meale would have pleas'd you noe lesse than it did me, as hardly consisting of one dish or glasse (besides bread and beere) of nearer growth than China, Persia, and the Cape of Good Hope." [43]

But it was now 1690, and increasingly difficult for these two friends to meet in Pepys' "little parlor," over a "dish of tripes," and share their "curious" pleasures. Pepys did not cease to write urgent letters, "Dear Sir, What shall I say more . . . than that we want you, wish for you, and pray for you?" [44] But Evelyn, since 1682, had been subject to "fits of an ague," which he accepted as a "warning and admonition" to "methodize all my writings, accounts, letters, and papers," expecting "Almighty God to call me from this transiatory life" at any moment. He was now less willing to leave the quiet of Sayes Court. For here was his garden, and here his library, where he considered himself very busy with his translation of La Quintyne's *Compleat Gardiner,* and with the assembling of material on medals for his *Numismata.* He was, moreover, quite content to pass his time "philosophising and world-despising in the solitudes of this place." To be sure, he regretted the absence of his "best and worthyest friend," but then he was reading Erasmus' *Praise of Folly,* and learning how to look down upon the world "with wondrous contempt." [45] Pepys replied that he took note of Evelyn's doctrine of despising the world, but wished to remind him that inasmuch as he loved "soe abject a clodd of it" as himself, he could not quite give it up. "Hasten then to towne," he pleaded again, "where wee have a whole summer's cropp of intelligence to gather," and also seed to put in the ground for another year. Evelyn's "weather-wisdome" was needed to judge what would come of the crop. "Hasten then to towne, and receive the longing wellcome of, Your most affectionate servant and honourer, S. Pepys."[46]

Though Evelyn seldom left his country retreat, in spite of these appeals, Pepys did not cease to consult him about his collections. "I want Mrs. Evelyn's head," he scribbled on September 25, 1690, "I am at a mighty losse for 2 or 3 other heads, the market not being able to furnish me therewith."[47] He was searching for the heads of old Admiral Nottingham, of the old Duke of Buckingham, my Lord Chancellor Clarendon, and his daughter the Duchess of York. "Pray see whether you have ever a head to spare of these." Evelyn answered the next day, supplying Pepys with one of the heads he asked for, that of Admiral Nottingham, and one he did not mention—his own.* "I send you, Sir, my face, such as it was *of yore,* but is now so *no more (tanto mutata).*"[48]

Pepys frequently sent Evelyn bundles of books from London. "This last packet of yours coming fruited with so many favours at once that I know not which of them first to give thanks for,"[49] wrote Evelyn in 1694. And again, "I thank you for the excellent book you sent me to peruse: there are many rare things, both in the cuts and in the discourse."[50] Evelyn was now taking great pleasure in "chewing-over some old stories, and among others the Reigne of *Lewes* the XIth, and *Charles Duke* of *Burgundy,*"[51] and enjoyed sharing his critical opinions with Pepys. "Now as for myselfe, I cannot but let you know the incredible satisfaction I have taken in reading my late Lord Chancellor's *History of the Rebellion,* so well, and so unexpectedly well written."[52] He referred to Locke's "addition to his excellent *Essay,*" and to a new book on *Religion and Reason,* which promised "an hours good diversion." Evelyn described to Pepys a visit from "the most learned Mr. Wotton," who brought with him as a present his *Reflections upon the Ancient and*

---

* See frontispiece.

Febr. 15. 169 4/5

Dearest S'^r

45

The Scent, as well as Noise, of Christmas now over with you (I presume) soe as a Man may Treate you in the bas stile againe.

Wee have had 2 great Vacancys fallen since wee last talk'd together; that in ye Church I am sure you & I shall thinke well fill'd; while the other in ye State fills it selfe. Fiat voluntas tua! And with this Interjection, lett mee give way, to an occasion that won't lett mee goe on, & I would not loose this Conveyance for ye small print that accompanys this, leabeing ye rest to a further but speedy Day. I bid you Adieu & am as allwayes

Yours indefinitely
Pepys.

LETTER FROM SAMUEL PEPYS TO JOHN EVELYN
February 15, 1695

Modern Learning. "Judge you then," he added, "what an unexpected blessing is befallen me in the wilderness, and with what *manna* I am fed." [53]

In his reply to Evelyn's letter, Pepys, who was also a friend of Wotton's, told Evelyn of this scholar's plan, "I mean, the reducing into less room what poor mankind is now to turn-over soe many cumbersome, jejune, and not seldom unintelligible volumes for," which he hoped Wotton would live to complete. "What a debt were this to lay upon mankind," [54] wrote Pepys, who, at least when corresponding with his studious friend in the country, sighed for a guide to a more universal knowledge than his genial attacks on the learned world had gained for him.

Evelyn, lost among his unfinished manuscripts on "The Sagacity of Brute Animals," the "Art of Stenography," "Medicinal Receipts," and "The History of Staves," was delighted by Pepys' report of Wotton's plan for reducing all knowledge to the essentials. He meditated upon the "monstrous lumber" through which one must struggle to come at last to any sort of knowledge, mathematical, botanical, historical, and theological.

What a benefactor were he, he wrote to Pepys in reply, that were able and willing to give us such a catalogue of authors as were onely, and absolutely, and fully effectual to the attaining of such a competency of practical, usefull, and speculative knowledge too, as one might hope to benefit by within the ordinarie circle of one's life, without being bewildered and quite out of the way when one should be gotten home.[55]

Evelyn himself was too frequently "bewildered and quite out of the way" in his circuitous route through "practical, useful, and speculative knowledge." Not long before he died Evelyn wrote in his *Memoires for my grand-son* of his "innumerable Insignificant Collections and Attempts, desultory and undigested, cast into no method," of his hundreds of authors marked with "my blak-lead Crayon," which he had intended to transcribe, of his translations, poems, "animadversions on Spinosa," which he had hoped to complete. "But had never leasure; In short—most, if not all, meere Embrios or Trifles, the mark of Time Indiscreetly lost and fit to be abolished, and are by me seriously Repented of." [56]

But one must not forget that from this laborious effort to encompass all knowledge there did emerge books on architecture, painting, libraries, numismatics, engraving, and gardening, which actually were guides and textbooks to his own generation. And though Evelyn often himself needed to be "gotten home," he was able, by his stores of learning and experienced taste, to direct and encourage Pepys, in assembling the "Bibliotheca Pepysiana."

VII

As absorbing a topic of conversation to Pepys and Evelyn as their libraries and collections was the question of religion, which besides causing political uneasiness to these supporters of James, excited their philosophical curiosity as members of the Royal Society. On September 15, 1685, Evelyn and Pepys "tooke coach and six horses, late after dinner," and drove to Portsmouth, where James was journeying, "to see in what state the fortifications were." We hear little from Evelyn's Diary of the fortifications, but we are told in detail of the conversation between the King and a group of noblemen and bishops which Pepys and Evelyn respectfully listened to the next morning when they waited on the King at Winchester. This remarkable conversation ranged from second sight to the cross of gold and amethysts found in Charles' pocket when he died; from ghosts to the healing powers of baptism. When His Majesty touched on miracles "and what strange things the Saludadors would do in Spaine," such as creeping into heated ovens without harm, Pepys listened with particular attention. He said nothing, however, for, as Evelyn explained in a footnote to the entry in his Diary, Pepys "did not conceive it fit to interrupt his Ma^{ty}, who so solemnly told what they pretended to do." Pepys told Evelyn later that, "being extreamly inquisitive of the truth of these pretended miracles," he himself when in Spain sought out a famous Saludador, and offered him a large reward if he would crawl into the hot oven before his eyes. The Saludador recognized that Pepys was "a more than ordinary curious person," and admitted that "he could do none of the feates really, but that what they pretended was all a cheate." One wonders what the effect would have been on James' conversation had Pepys "conceived it fit" to express what was in his mind.

Several weeks later Pepys held another long conversation with King James, which moved him to write a hasty note to Evelyn, on October 2, urging him to dine with him that same evening, for "I have something to shew you that I may not have another time." "I accordingly went," Evelyn recorded in his Diary. After dinner Pepys ushered Evelyn and Mr. Houblon, his other guest, into a private room, and told them in confidence of the conversation he had lately held with His Majesty, King James, which at last turned upon "my late Lord Arlington dying a Roman Catholic, who had all along seemed to profess himselfe a Protestant."

This familiar discourse encourag'd Mr. Pepys to beg of his Ma^{ty}, if he might ask it without offence, and for that his Ma^{ty} could not but observe how it was whisper'd among many, whether his late Ma^{ty} had ben reconcil'd to ye Church of Rome; he againe humbly besought his Ma^{ty} to pardon his presumption if he had touch'd upon a thing which did not befit him to looke into.

The King told Pepys candidly that Charles was during his life a Catholic, and died in that belief. He then led him into his closet, and there drew forth from a cabinet two papers, written in Charles' own hand, attesting his faith in the Catholic Church. His Majesty was glad to lend Pepys copies of the papers, and these were the documents Evelyn saw and read that evening in York Buildings. "I was heartily sorry to see all this," he added, "tho' it was no other than was to be suspected, by his late Ma^{tys} too greate indifference, neglect, and course of life, that he had been perverted."

Though Pepys might have been secretly delighted with himself for having these two papers of King James, one cannot doubt that Evelyn was, indeed, "heartily sorry to see all this." For Evelyn had remained an ardent Church of England man during the time of the Commonwealth, and during the troubled reigns of Charles and James, when "all engines" were "at work to bring in Popery wch God in mercy prevent." At the time of the Commonwealth, services had ceased in the parish churches; Evelyn, therefore, had "frequently stay'd at home to chatechise and instruct" [57] his family. After the

Church of England clergy were forbidden to preach or administer the Sacraments, Evelyn observed in his household "a solemn fast for ye calamity of our Church." He patiently accepted the death of eight of his nine children as just chastisement inflicted on his wife and himself for their sins, and on each anniversary of his birth he resolved to give himself up more entirely to God. Now, after reading Charles' confession of faith in the Catholic Church, he did not hesitate to conclude that

God was incens'd to make his reign very troublesome and unprosperous, by warrs, plagues, fires, losse of reputation by an universal neglect of the publique for the love of a voluptuous and sensual life, wch a vicious Court had brought into credit.

Evelyn himself would probably have been surprised had he known how much less ardently Pepys looked upon questions of religion. He too attempted family prayers, but on Michaelmas Day, 1661, and probably on other occasions, too, he was "even almost foxed," so that he "durst not read prayers, for fear of being perceived by [his] servants in what case [he] was." Pepys, as well as Evelyn, made devout appeals to God, especially when he came to his final reckonings at the end of the year. But far from giving himself up entirely to the Lord, as Evelyn wished to do, Pepys was apt to reflect in his Diary upon the fact that "all these things are ordered by God Almighty to make me contented." [58] Pepys was as shocked as Evelyn to see the courtiers at Whitehall playing cards on Sunday, and at least attended church with respectable frequency. But he carried his "perspective glasses" with him to turn upon the ladies of the congregation when he was doomed to listen to "a lazy, simple sermon," and if he was bored, he went from one church to another, "hearing a bit here and a bit there." One wonders what Evelyn made of Pepys' exit when he drove

. . . with Sir Richard Browne and Mr. Evelyn, in their coach to the church, where Mr. Plume preached. But I, in the midst of the sermon, did go out, and walked all alone to Deptford, thinking para have seen the wife of Bagwell, which I did at her door, but I could not conveniently go into her house, and so lost my labour.[59]

Pepys certainly did not regard the copies of Charles' confession of faith with Evelyn's distress. He probably looked upon them as very interesting political documents. For he himself, closely associated with the Duke of York, had on more than one occasion been accused of Papacy, and had, as we know, not many years before this particular evening, been put in the Tower on a baseless charge of a connection with the Popish Plot, from which he was completely exonerated after a year's imprisonment. Though Pepys secured a letter from his wife's brother, and from Dr. Milles, the minister of St. Olave's church, testifying that his wife, the daughter of a French Huguenot, died a Protestant, the rumor that Mrs. Pepys was at heart a Catholic never ceased to trouble him. During her life, Pepys was himself not certain of his wife's religion. On November 29, 1668, he recorded in his Diary that he was "in much fear of what she lately frighted me with about her being a Catholique." Several weeks later we read that he was mightily pleased when she accompanied him to church, "I being full of fear that she would never go to church again, after she had declared to me that she was a Roman Catholique." [60] No wonder that he needed support of a letter from her brother and Dr. Milles after the death of his wife.

Evelyn's attitude towards the danger to England of the Roman Catholic Church was made perfectly clear when, on May 12, 1686, as Commissioner of the Privy Seal, he refused to "put the Privy Seale to Dr. Walker's licence for printing and publishing divers Popish books." Needless to say, Evelyn soon lost his position. But he continued to watch the political-religious situation very closely, being on intimate terms with the leading ecclesiastics of the day. In 1687, his friend Sancroft and six other bishops refused to read the Declaration of Indulgence, granting Papists and Dissenters freedom of worship, and were sent to the Tower. Evelyn visited them there, and joined in the public rejoicing at their release several months later. In the following year, when the church's attitude towards William was under discussion, Evelyn was invited to a conference of churchmen at Lambeth where he listened with concern to the many different opinions discussed. His friend Archbishop Sancroft refused to take the oath of allegiance to William, and was therefore suspended. Evelyn continued to visit his old and broken friend in his dismantled house, when he was waiting to receive his summons to leave.

Evelyn was troubled, too, in this year of revolution, for his friend Pepys, who had been at this time sent to the Gatehouse on vague accusations of being still friendly to James and of selling naval secrets to the French. The accusation was so unsupported that he was retained only five days. But the political significance of religious beliefs must have been very present in the minds of those who attended Mr. Pepys' dinner party during this dangerous period.

I din'd with Mr. Pepys, [wrote Evelyn] where was Dr. Cumberland the new Bishop of Norwich, Dr. Lloyd having been put out for not acknowledging the Government. Cumberland is a very learned, excellent man.—Possession was now given to Dr. Tillotson at Lambeth, by the Sheriff; Abp. Sancroft was gon, but he had left his nephew to keepe possession; and he refusing to deliver it up on the Queene's message, was dispossess'd by ye Sheriff and imprison'd. This stout demeanor of the few Bishops who refus'd to take the oaths to K. William, animated a greate party to forsake the churches, so as to threaten a schisme.[61]

Evelyn was friendly with Tillotson, who succeeded Sancroft as Archbishop of Canterbury, and with Tenison, "my dear and particular friend," who succeeded Tillotson. Dining with archbishops became, indeed, his especial pleasure. The elaborate formality, orthodox piety, scholarly learning, and worldly taste, which marked the evenings of conversation passed among the bishops, must have been reassuring to the aristocratic Evelyn in these troubled times. "I din'd at Lambeth," he wrote, "making my first visite to the Archbishop, where there was much company and great cheere. After prayers in the evening, my Lord made me stay to shew me his house, furniture and garden, wch were all very fine." [62]

Not only did Evelyn enjoy the elegance of archbishops' palaces, and the prestige of "much private and free discourse" with these dignitaries concerning the political situation, but he also entered with zeal into more remote discussions of the mysteries of the church. "I then went with the Bp. of St. Asaph to the Abp. of Lambeth," he wrote on April 26, 1689, "where they enter'd into discourse concerning the final destruction of Antichrist, both concluding that the third trumpet and vial were now pouring out." On a later visit this "prophesying Bishop" proved from the Apocalypse that the French King's ruin was near at hand, and that the Kingdom of Antichrist would be entirely destroyed within thirty years, when "the true religion and universal peace should obtain thro' all the world." [63]

Pepys was at this time in the Gatehouse. But he had been released scarcely two weeks before he received a note from Evelyn inviting him to share in these remarkable conversations.

Sir, This hasty script is to acquaint you that my Lord Bishop of St Asaph will take it for an honour to be thought able to give Mr. Pepys any light in those mysteries you and I have discoursed of.[64]

The next day Evelyn merely noted down in his Diary that "The Bp. of St Asaph expounds his prophecies to me and Mr. Pepys, etc." We can imagine with what interest he and Pepys heard the political and religious future of Europe read from the Apocalypse.

VIII

Not many years after this evening spent with the Bishop of St. Asaph, both Pepys and Evelyn were forced, by age and illness, to retire to their country estates, Pepys to Clapham in 1700, and Evelyn to Wotton at about the same time. Now Evelyn was moved to "serious reflections." Though these two friends had shared many interests and pleasures, Evelyn was forced sorrowfully to conclude in a letter to Pepys of August 9, 1700, that all was illusion. "The scantinesse, mutabillity, and little satisfaction of the things of this world, after all our reserches in quest of something we think worth the paines," only proved, he wrote to Pepys, that we were pursuing "images." Now we should take warning that "there is another and a better state of things which concerne us, and for which I pray Almighty God to prepare us both." [65]

In spite of this other and better state for which Evelyn was preparing, one observes that his present state, in the extensive family home of Wotton, was pleasant indeed. In 1694 he had moved his family from Sayes Court to Wotton to join his aging brother George. Evelyn at once began to make more beautiful the garden he had helped set out many years earlier. "I am planting an ever-green grove here to an old house ready to drop," he wrote to his friend Dr. Bohun. Here he and his family had a private apartment of five rooms, and a "pretty closet," where he collected "the spoiles of Sayes Court . . . now the raree-shew of the neighborhood." His "good old Brother" enjoyed country customs and, at this particular Christmas season, entertained "no fewer than 300 bumpkins." Wednesday and Saturday nights were "Lecture Nights," when Evelyn and his wife read aloud the news packet sent down from London, which served them "for discourse till fresh newes" came. Such was the history "of a very old man and his no young companion," whose society he was now enjoying more than he was ever before able to during the fifty years of their married life. But, in spite of these country contentments, Evelyn never allowed himself to forget that he was every day "trussing up to be gon,"[66] he hoped to a better place.

In 1699, the same year that Evelyn published *Acetoria, a Discourse of Sallets,* it was his brother George and his one remaining son, John, who moved to a "better place," leaving him with but one surviving child, Suzanna. Evelyn inherited Wotton at last, and devoted his attention, not unhappily, to the pruning of his evergreens, and the rearing of his grandson, John. Life went on at Wotton much as before. "You will now inquire what I do here?" he wrote to Pepys on July 22, 1700:

Why! as the Patriarches of old, I passe the day in the fields, among horses and oxen, sheep and cowes, bulls and sows, *et cetera pecora campi.* . . . This without. Now within-dores. Never was any matron more buisy than my wife, disposing of our plaine country furniture for a naked old extravagant house, suitable to our imployments. . . . But can you thus hold-out, will my friend say? Is Philosophy, Gr[esham] Coll[ege], and the example of Mr. Pepys and agreable conversation of Yorke buildings, quite forgotten and abandoned? No, no. . . . Know that I have ben ranging of no fewer than 30 large cases of books, destined for a competent standing library during 5 or six days.[67]

Pepys wrote back to Evelyn from "Paradisial Clapham," where, Evelyn told us after one of his infrequent visits, "he has a very noble and wonderfully well furnish'd house, especially with India and Chinese curiosities,"[68] that, as for him, he had no herds to mind, nor would his doctor allow him any books. "'What then,' will you say too, 'are you a doing?'" In truth, said Pepys, nothing that can be named. And yet he was not idle, for who can be idle who has so much to think over, "of past and to come," as had Pepys? "And thinking, I take it," he added, with perhaps a touch of irony, "is working; though many formes beneath what my Lady and you are a doing." "But pray remember," he finished, "what a clock it is with you and me," and do not now be over bold with "your *strangury,* any more than I dare be with my *stone.*" [69]

The next month, in spite of Evelyn's "strangury," he and his lady, "with their whole family of children, children-in-law and grandchildren" did make a trip to Clapham to call on Pepys. Evelyn hoped that "the sweete breath of our Surry downes [would] tempt you to descend so low as your most faithfull, humble servants." [70] But Pepys, too infirm to venture so far as the Surrey downs, was left at Clapham to mourn the lack of his old friends, "and at the head of them all, the most inestimable Mr. Evelyn." One way or another, Pepys hoped they would see each other before the winter was over, "and possibly a great many other sights that we don't think of." [71]

Evelyn's health did, indeed, allow him to spend a few months of that winter of 1701 in the "smoaky, obstreperous Citty" of London, in the empty home of his son John. Evelyn remembered with sadness, as he made his way along Whitehall, the days when he and Pepys were able fully to share in the life of London. "In good earnest, Sir," he wrote to Pepys on December 10, 1701,

I passe not by Yorke-Buildings without serious regrets. *Saturday,* which was wont to be a *Jubily,* and the most advantagious and gainefull, as well as the most diverting to me of the Weekely Circles, is from a real *Sabbath* and day of repose now become wholy saturnine, lugubrous and solitary.[72]

Exchange of useful information on barley waters, emulsions of almonds, and the wonders of "nephretic powders described in yesterday's *Flying Post*" was a poor substitute for dinners in York Buildings.* Even news of Evelyn's "young Scholar," his virtuous

---

* The two following entries in Evelyn's Diary suggest that Pepys and Evelyn had long enjoyed consultations over their health and that of their families.
June 10, 1669, "I went this evening to London, to carry Mr. Pepys to my Brother Rich[d], now exceedingly afflicted with the stone, who had been successfully cut, and carried the stone as big as a tennis-ball, to shew him and encourage his resolution to go thro' the operation." March 2, 1682, "Came to see and congratulate my recovery, S[r]. John Lowther, Mr. Herbert, Mr. Pepys, Sir Anth. Deane, and Mr. Hill."

grandson, who was busy with his mathematics, but "forgets not the greate respect he owes to you," could be little comfort to Pepys. The epigrams and Latin poems written by this serious Oxonian, which Evelyn copied out and enclosed in his letters to Pepys, did, however, offer Pepys, in turn, an excuse for venturing "at entertaining you with something from my *young-man* [John Jackson] in exchange (I don't say in payment) for the pleasure you gratify me with from *yours*." [73] Pepys enclosed in his letter a list of the prints brought back to him by John Jackson at the end of his two-year tour of Europe, and asked for Evelyn's comment on his "Roman markettings." Evelyn wished very much to participate in the "cargo" Pepys' "accomplished nephew" had happily brought home, but, indeed, Evelyn's taste for "things superfluous" was very different from what it had been.

For each fresh attack of illness Evelyn took as a gracious advertisement from God that he must prepare for his "latter end," which at his age could not be far off. He wished, he said, to be ready with his "packet" when his day arrived. He reminded Pepys of Epictetus' saying, that, when the master summons the passengers on board the ship, they must leave their cockleshells on the shore and obey. "This alarme, Friend, is frequently in my thoughts," he added, intent though he still was "upon finishing of a thousand impertinencys which I fancy would render my habitation, my library, garden, collections, and the worke I am about, compleate and easy." [74] But they must both be ready to leave all of these "impertinencys" when the Master should call. Indeed Evelyn, who in 1702 became a member of the Society for the Propagation of the Gospel in Foreign Parts, was all too apt in writing to Pepys to fall into a sermon rather than a letter. His mind continually turned to

the vessel and the voyage which, through all these tempests and tossings here, shall (I trust) set us safe on shore in those regions of peace and love and lasting friendships, and where those whose refined and exalted nature makes capable of the sublimest mysterys, and aspire after experimental knowledge (truely so called), shall be filled; and there without danger tast of the Fruite of the Tree (which cost our unhapy parents so deare); shall meete with no prohibition of what is desierable, no serpent to deceive, none to be deceived. This is, Sir, the state of that

Royal Society above, and of those who shall be the worthy members of it.[75]

Pepys' nature, never quite so "refined and exalted" as Evelyn's, was unable to join him in this flight to "those regions of peace and love and lasting friendship."

What then should I have to say to the whole of that glorious matter that was so enclosed in your last? Why truly, neither more nor less than that it looks to me like a seraphick *How d'ye* from one already entered into the regions you talk of in it, and who has sent me this for a *viaticum* towards my speeding thither after him.[76]

As a matter of fact, Pepys sped to their next place of meeting three years in advance of Evelyn. John Jackson wrote to Evelyn, on the evening of May 28, 1703, just two weeks after his last call at Clapham: *

Honoured Sir, 'Tis no small addition to my grief, to be obliged to interrupt the quiet of your happy recess with the afflicting tidings of my uncle Pepys's death, knowing how sensibly you will partake with me herein.[77]

Evelyn was sent the mourning ring; he was asked to help hold up the pall, but being an old man and ill, he had to refuse. He contented himself, instead, with writing in his Diary, a summary of what Pepys stood for in his mind.

This day died Mr. Sam. Pepys, a very worthy, industrious and curious person, none in England exceeding him in knowledge of the navy, in wch he had passed thro' all the most considerable offices, Clerk of the Acts and Secretary of the Admiralty, all wch he perform'd with great integrity. When K. James II. went out of England, he laid down his office, and would serve no more, but withdrawing himselfe from all public affairs, he liv'd at Clapham with his partner Mr. Hewer, formerly his clerk, in a very noble house and sweete place, where he

---

* Sir Arthur Ponsonby, in *John Evelyn* (London, 1933), supplies us with the note from Evelyn's Diary which is omitted from all printed texts. May 14, 1703, "I called in also at Clapham to visit Mr. Pepys now languishing with smallpox which much affected me." Quoted from *The Abinger Monthly Record*, July, 1889.

enjoy'd the fruite of his labours in greate prosperity. He was universally belov'd, hospitable, generous, learned in many things, skill'd in music, a very greate cherisher of learned men of whom he had the conversation. His library and collection of other curiosities were of the most considerable, the models of ships especially. Besides what he publish'd of an account of the Navy, as he found and left it, he had for divers yeares under his hand the History of the Navy, or *Navalia* as he call'd it; but how far advanc'd, and what will follow of his, is left, I suppose, to his sister's son Mr. Jackson, a young gentleman whom Mr. Pepys had educated in all sorts of usefull learning, sending him to travel abroad, from whence he return'd with extraordinary accomplishments, and worthy to be heir. Mr. Pepys had been for neere 40 yeares so much my particular friend, that Mr. Jackson sent me compleat mourning, desiring me to be one to hold up the pall at his magnificent obsequies, but my indisposition hinder'd me from doing him this last office.[78]

It is pleasant to think that after these forty years of experiences shared during the stormy time of Charles, James, and William that Evelyn knew, or at least recorded, nothing more of Pepys than that he was a "worthy, industrious and curious person," remarkable for his "knowledge of the navy," and for his "library and collection of other curiosities." Perhaps it was this very quality of detachment which made it possible for these two men, the one an ardent Church of England Royalist, a scholar, and a dilettante, the other an ambitious politician and pragmatic churchman, to associate with each other, through so many turns of fortune, with mutual respect and pleasure. Pepys' enterprise and industry enabled him to achieve a position of great power as the organizing force behind the English Navy in the time of the Dutch Wars; Evelyn's tireless curiosity and experienced artistic sense won him a place of authority among the most eminent scientists, poets, and divines of his day. Without this instructive friendship it is possible that Pepys would never have assembled the collections of books and prints we enjoy today in the library at Magdalene College, that Evelyn would have lost himself even more hopelessly among his evergreen hedges and unfinished manuscripts at Sayes Court and Wotton. Both Pepys and Evelyn knew how to enjoy tastes and temperaments somewhat different from their own, and understood the rules of friendship,

PRIVATE ENJOYMENT   73

not the least important of which Evelyn wrote in his *Memoires for my grand-son*. "Whether it be to Friend or Foe, talk not other men's lives & faults, and reveale them not." [79] Evelyn at least extended this excellent rule to include what he wrote of Pepys in his Diary; his references to him are without exception impersonal and objective, though we know from his letters to Pepys that he looked upon him with great personal affection. Whether this affection was based on anything more than a very partial knowledge of Pepys' character, we may well doubt. An anonymous friend of Evelyn's wrote soon after his death, "He was a gentleman of a character highly respectable in every view." Though austere in temperament, he was possessed of the "most elegant and useful accomplishments, and blessed with the most amiable virtues." [80] It was probably these qualities in the somewhat aloof Evelyn which endeared him to Pepys.

That Evelyn's relationship with Pepys, was, however, always controlled by the moderation and good sense of the Age of Reason is suggested by a brief exchange of letters, which was soon to pass between Evelyn and John Jackson, Pepys' heir and adopted son, and between Evelyn and Mr. Hewer, Pepys' secretary and lifelong friend. Two years after the death of Pepys, John Jackson desired to lay all his "useful knowledge" and "extraordinary accomplishments," so much admired by Evelyn, at the feet of Evelyn's granddaughter, thus joining forever the families of Evelyn and Pepys. Evelyn, however, suspected that Pepys had left a good portion of his £12,000 to Mrs. Skinner, who had been his housekeeper and mistress since 1670. He made polite inquiries of Mr. Hewer, found that his suspicions were justified, and gently withdrew from the difficult situation with the following note to Mr. Jackson, a corrected, interlined and much worked-over copy of which is to be seen among the Evelyn manuscripts in the British Museum.

S^r, I should be most sensibly touch'd, did any thing of this Proposal receive the least interruption from me or my Wife, who shall ever esteeme Mr Jackson's Person & extraordinary Accomplishments of far more Value than his Estate, were it a great deale more and am therefore most heartily Sorry, that those Circumstances (according to the Custome & Interests of this Age, and the Satisfaction of Relations) should interrupt its farther progresse.[81]

One cannot doubt that Pepys himself, who went to so much trouble to secure a substantial marriage portion for his sister Pauline, the mother of John Jackson, would have entirely sympathized both with Evelyn's decision and with the graceful urbanity of his note to the dismissed suitor. For Pepys would have subscribed to another maxim which Evelyn wrote for the guidance of his grandson, "Avoyd Extremes & be ever provided with some laudable excuse," [82] a maxim which these two gentlemen unconsciously obeyed in their long and always rewarding friendship.

Notes

INTRODUCTION

1. *The Diary of Samuel Pepys.* Edited with Additions by Henry B. Wheatley, F. S. A.; London (1892), December 21, 1665. (The quotations in the text are from Wheatley's edition of Pepys' Diary, rather than from Braybrooke's, since Wheatley's is somewhat more accurate.)
2. See Appendix, pp. 83–84
3. *The Diary of John Evelyn, Esq., F. R. S.* To which are added a Selection from his Familiar Letters. . . . Edited by William Bray. A new edition in four volumes by Henry B. Wheatley, London (1906), July 20, 1685
4. *Ibid.,* January 16, 1679
5. *Ibid.,* June 4, 1679
6. *The Diary and Correspondence of Samuel Pepys, Esq., F. R. S.* . . . with a Life and Notes by Richard, Lord Braybrooke, London (1876) IV, 303-4
7. Richard Hone, *Lives of Eminent Christians,* 2 vols., London (1836), p. 201
8. *Private Correspondence and Miscellaneous Papers of Samuel Pepys, 1679–1703.* Edited by J. R. Tanner, 2 vols., London (1926), I, 378
9. *Ibid.,* I, 23
10. *Letters and Second Diary of Samuel Pepys.* Edited by R. G. Howarth, London (1932), p. 334
11. Pepys' *Correspondence,* Tanner, I, 133
12. Pepys' *Diary,* November 5, 1665

CHAPTER I

I.

1. Pepys' *Diary,* August 20, 1662
2. *Ibid.,* November 24, 1665
3. *Ibid.,* September 18, 1665
4. *Ibid.,* October 13, 1665
5. *Ibid.,* October 6, 1665
6. *Ibid.,* October 19, 1665
7. *Ibid.,* September 23, 1665
8. *Ibid.,* September 25, 1665

II.

9. See Appendix, p. 86
10. Pepys' *Diary,* September 23, 1665

11. See Appendix, p. 87
12. *Ibid.*, p. 88
13. *Further Correspondence of Samuel Pepys, 1662–1679.* Edited by J. R. Tanner. London (1929), p. 116
14. Pepys' *Diary*, January 29, 1666
15. *Ibid.*, February 20, 1666
16. Evelyn's *Diary*, February 20, 1666
17. Pepys' *Diary*, February 20, 1666
18. *Ibid.*, October 5, 1665

III.

19. Evelyn's *Diary*, September 7, 1665
20. Pepys' *Diary*, September 20, 1665
21. *Ibid.*, August 30, 1665
22. *Ibid.*, October 5, 1665
23. *Ibid.*, August 31, 1665
24. *Ibid.*, August 9, 1666

IV.

25. Evelyn's *Diary*, January 29, 1666
26. Pepys' *Diary*, September 3, 1666
27. Evelyn's *Diary*, September 3, 1666
28. John Evelyn, *Fumifugium*, London, 1661 (1929), p. 8

V.

29. Pepys' *Diary*, September 26, 1666
30. *Ibid.*, December 14, 1666
31. *Ibid.*, April 26, 1667
32. *Ibid.*, June 3, 1667
33. *Ibid.*, August 8, 1667
34. *Ibid.*, November 30, 1667
35. *Ibid.*, March 16, 1669
36. Evelyn's *Diary*, April 30, 1663
37. *Ibid.*, February 4, 1685
38. *Ibid.*, May 3, 1660
39. *Ibid.*, November 7, 1659
40. *Ibid.*, March 1, 1671
41. *Ibid.*, October 1, 1661
42. *Ibid.*, May 5, 1670. See Arthur Ponsonby, *John Evelyn*, London (1933), p. 69
43. *Ibid.*, May 14, 1661
44. *Ibid.*, August 14, 1668
45. *Ibid.*, April 23, 1661

VI.

46. Pepys' *Diary*, June 16, 1667
47. *Ibid.*, June 19, 1667
48. Pepys' *Letters*, Howarth, p. 32

VII.

49. Evelyn's *Diary*, August 21, 1674

50. See Appendix, p. 117
51. Pepys' *Diary*, January 28, 1666
52. Pepys' *Letters*, Howarth, p. 144
53. *Ibid.*, pp. 151–2
54. *Ibid.*, pp. 152–3
55. See Appendix, p. 140
56. Pepys' *Letters*, Howarth, p. 198

VIII.

57. Evelyn's *Diary*, March 7, 1690
58. *Memoirs of Samuel Pepys, Esq., F. R. S.* . . . comprising his Diary from 1659 to 1669 . . . and a Selection from his Private Correspondence. Edited by Richard, Lord Braybrooke. 2 vols. London (1825), II, 108
59. *Admiralty Letters*, x, 170. Quoted by J. R. Tanner, *Pepys Memoires of the Royal Navy 1679–1688*, Oxford (1906), XIII
60. Pepys' *Letters*, Howarth, p. 219
61. Evelyn's *Diary*, June 10, 1690
62. Pepys' *Correspondence*, Tanner, I, 31
63. *Ibid.*, I, 29–30
64. Evelyn's *Diary*, June 24, 1690
65. *Ibid.*
66. *Ibid.*, July 30, 1690
67. Pepys' *Memoires*, Braybrooke, II, 112
68. Pepys' *Letters*, Howarth, p. 266
69. Pepys' *Diary*, November 24, 1665
70. Evelyn's *Diary*, August 28, 1670
71. Evelyn, *Letters*, Bray, III, 381
72. John Evelyn, *Navigation and Commerce*, London (1674), p. 17
73. *Ibid.*, p. 61
74. Pepys' *Correspondence*, Tanner, I, 22
75. *Ibid.*, I, 15
76. *Ibid.*, pp. 14–18
77. Evelyn's *Diary*, January 28, 1682
78. *Ibid.*, June 2, 1672
79. See Appendix, p. 122
80. *Ibid.*, 132
81. Pepys' *Correspondence*, Tanner, I, pp. 14–15
82. See Appendix, p. 132
83. Evelyn's *Letters*, Bray, III, 414
84. See Appendix, pp. 115–116
85. *Ibid.*, pp. 120–121
86. *Ibid.*, p. 120
87. *Ibid.*, p. 122
88. *Ibid.*, p. 125
89. Evelyn's *Letters*, Bray, III, 420
90. Appendix, pp. 150–151
91. J. R. Tanner, *Mr. Pepys*, London (1925), p. 280
92. Evelyn's *Diary*, May 26, 1703

CHAPTER II

I.
1. Pepys' *Diary*, September 10, 1665
2. Evelyn's *Diary*, June 13, 1651
3. Evelyn's *Letters*, Bray, IV, 22
4. *Ibid.*, III, 262
5. *Ibid.*, p. 266
6. John Evelyn, *Sculptura*, London (1755), p. XXXI
7. John Evelyn, translation of Naudés' *Instructions for Erecting of a Library*, Cambridge (1903), Dedication, xvii–xviii

II.
8. Thomas Birch, *History of the Royal Society*, London (1754), IV, 429
9. *Ibid.*, p. 425
10. Evelyn's *Diary*, December 13, 1685
11. *Ibid.*, August 26, 1676
12. *Ibid.*, August 6, 1698
13. *Ibid.*, May 30, 1698
14. *Ibid.*, January 27, 1689
15. Pepys' *Correspondence*, Tanner, II, 302
16. Evelyn's *Diary*, February 19, 1671
17. Pepys' *Correspondence*, Tanner, I, 59
18. Pepys' *Diary*, April 29, 1666. See also Pepys' *Diary*, May 1, 1665; May 5, 1665; December 17, 1665

III.
19. Quoted by Hone, *Op. cit.*, p. 166
20. Pepys' *Letters*, Howarth, p. 35
21. *Ibid.*, p. 36
22. See *frontispiece*
23. Pepys' *Letters*, Howarth, p. 37
24. See Appendix, pp. 101–102
25. Pepys' *Letters*, Howarth, p. 37
26. Pepys' *Correspondence*, Tanner, II, 242–3

IV.
27. Davey Catalogue, London (1889), Item no. 2884
28. Pepys' *Diary*, November 3, 1665
29. *Ibid.*, October 5, 1665
30. Evelyn's *Diary*, January 11, 1694
31. *Ibid.*, October 18, 1666
32. *Ibid.*, November 26, 1661
33. Pepys' *Letters*, Howarth, p. 186
34. Pepys' *Diary*, November 5, 1665

V.
35. Evelyn's *Diary*, July 23, 1678
36. *Ibid.*, September 13, 1687

NOTES 79

37. *Ibid.*, February 15, 1684
38. Evelyn's *Letters*, Bray, III, 436
39. *Ibid.*
40. *Ibid.*, p. 457

VI

41. Pepys' *Correspondence*, Tanner, I, 287
42. *Ibid.*, II, 3
43. Pepys' *Letters*, Howarth, 222
44. *Ibid.*, p. 240
45. Pepys' *Correspondence*, Tanner, I, 59
46. *Ibid.*, pp. 62–63
47. Howarth, p. 219
48. Pepys' *Correspondence*, Tanner, I, 34
49. *Ibid.*, I, 99
50. Pepys' *Letters*, Howarth, p. 272
51. Pepys' *Correspondence*, Tanner, I, 133
52. *Ibid.*, II, 301
53. *Ibid.*, I, 95
54. *Ibid.*, p. 97
55. *Ibid.*, pp. 100–1
56. *Memoires for my grand-son*, edited by Geoffrey Keynes, London (1926), p. 68

VII

57. Evelyn's *Diary*, September 19, 1655
58. Pepys' *Diary*, July 26, 1665
59. *Ibid.*, March 29, 1669
60. *Ibid.*, December 6, 1668
61. Evelyn's *Diary*, July 11, 1691
62. *Ibid.*, July 6, 1695
63. *Ibid.*, June 18, 1690
64. Pepys' *Correspondence*, Tanner, I, 33

VIII

65. *Ibid.*, II, 38
66. Evelyn's *Letters*, Bray, III, 136 (footnote)
67. Pepys' *Correspondence*, Tanner, II, 20
68. Evelyn's *Diary*, September 23, 1700
69. Pepys' *Correspondence*, Tanner, II, 35–36
70. *Ibid.*, I, 343
71. Pepys' *Letters*, Howarth, p. 334
72. Pepys' *Correspondence*, Tanner, II, 237
73. *Ibid.*, II, 36
74. *Ibid.*, p. 38
75. *Ibid.*, p. 238–9
76. *Ibid.*, p. 241
77. Pepys' *Letters*, Howarth, p. 374
78. Evelyn's *Diary*, May 26, 1703

79. *Op. Cit.*, p. 80
80. Add. MS 15. 951, f. 27
81. See Appendix, pp. 144–145
82. *Memoires for my grand-son*, p. 79

APPENDIX

I. Manuscript Letters
        Pepys-Evelyn
        Hewer-Evelyn
        Jackson-Evelyn

II. Finding List of Letters Advertised in Book
       Catalogues

III. Finding List of Printed Letters

Appendix

WE know that Pepys and Evelyn exchanged at least 127 letters in the course of their long friendship. Of this number thirty-seven letters are printed for the first time in Section I of this Appendix; twenty-three, the location of which is now unknown, are listed in the sales catalogues of various bookdealers, and are often accompanied with photographs or excerpts (see Section II); two are noted in the Reports of the Historical Manuscripts Commission, but their contents are not summarized; eight are in the possession of Mr. Carl Pforzheimer of New York City; fifty-seven have been printed and are most easily accessible in the following editions of the Pepys and Evelyn correspondence:

Memoires of Samuel Pepys, Esq., F.R.S. . . . comprising his Diary from 1659 to 1669 . . . and a Selection from his private Correspondence. Edited by Richard, Lord Braybrooke. 2 vols., London, 1825

Diary and Correspondence of Samuel Pepys, Esq., F.R.S. . . . with a Life and Notes by Richard, Lord Braybrooke. Deciphered with additional notes by Rev. Mynors Bright, M.A. 6 vols., London, 1875-79

Private Correspondence and Miscellaneous Papers of Samuel Pepys, 1679-1703. Edited by J. L. Tanner. 2 vols., London, 1926

Further Correspondence of Samuel Pepys, 1662-1679. Edited by J. R. Tanner. London, 1929

Letters and The Second Diary of Samuel Pepys. Edited by R. G. Howarth. London, 1932

The Diary of John Evelyn, Esq., F.R.S. To which are added a Selection from his Familiar Letters . . . edited by William Bray. A new edition in four volumes by Henry B. Wheatley, London, 1906

Of the thirty-seven unpublished letters, which I have been able to add to the Pepys-Evelyn collection, twenty-six are in the handwriting of Pepys and Evelyn, and eleven are copies of letters made by Pepys' secretaries. Two unpublished letters written to Evelyn by John Jackson and William Hewer, after Pepys' death, and two drafts of Evelyn's replies might well be considered a part of this correspondence. They also are printed in the following Appendix, Section I. The manuscripts of these letters are to be found in the British Museum, the Bodleian, the Public Record Office, the Pepsian Library, the Morgan Library, the Huntington Library, the Library of the Historical Society of Pennsylvania, and in the collection of Dr. Rosenbach of Philadelphia.

Mr. Carl Pforzheimer, of New York City, has in his possession eight letters exchanged by Pepys and Evelyn in the year 1699, four written by Pepys and four by Evelyn. Though he allowed me to see these letters, he has not permitted me to study them in detail or to print their exact dates. Nor have I been able to obtain permission to study the Evelyn manuscripts, still in the possession of the Evelyn family at Wotton, which would probably greatly enlarge our understanding of the Pepys-Evelyn relationship.

Our knowledge of the friendship of the two diarists must remain, for the present, incomplete. In Sections I, II, and III of this Appendix, I am offering a tentative list of the letters exchanged by Pepys and Evelyn.

SECTION I

Manuscript Letters

Abbreviations Used: British Museum (BM); Bodleian Library (BL); English Public Record Office (EPRO); Pepysian Library (PL); Morgan Library (ML); Huntington Library (HL); Historical Society of Pennsylvania (HSP); Collection of Dr. Rosenbach (R)

In the following list I have used the new style for all dates between January 1 and March 25.

		page
1. Evelyn to Pepys—September 23, 1665—EPRO S. P. 29/133 f. 28—		86
2. ——————————September 29, 1665—EPRO S. P. 29/133 f. 58—		87
3. ——————————September 30, 1665—EPRO S. P. 29/133 f. 63—		87

APPENDIX 85

				page
4.	————————	—October 3, 1665	—EPRO S. P. 29/134 ff. 23–24—	89
5.	————————	—October 13, 1665	—EPRO S. P. 29/134 f. 85—	92
6.	————————	—October 14, 1665	—EPRO S. P. 29/134 f. 93—	92
7.	————————	—October 23, 1665	—EPRO S. P. 29/135 f. 44—	93
8.	————————	—November 4, 1665	—EPRO S. P. 29/136 f. 31—	94
9.	————————	—November 23, 1665	—EPRO S. P. 29/137 f. 84—	94
10.	————————	—December 7, 1665	—EPRO S. P. 29/138 f. 60—	95
11.	————————	—December 9, 1665	—EPRO S. P. 29/138 f. 77—	96
12.	Pepys to Evelyn	—December 12, 1665	—ML—	97
13.	Evelyn to Pepys	—December 13, 1665	—EPRO S. P. 29/139 f. 11—	97
14.	————————	—January 31, 1666	—EPRO S. P. 29/146 f. 73—	98
15.	————————	—February 17, 1666	—EPRO S. P. 29/146 f. 51—	99
16.	————————	—February 28, 1666	—EPRO S. P. 29/149 f. 59—	99
17.	————————	—March 16, 1666	—EPRO S. P. 29/151 f. 35—	100
18.	————————	—August 21, 1669	—PL MSS 2237—	101
19.	————————	—August 27, 1672	—EPRO S. P. 29/328 f. 114—	109
20.	————————	—September 20, 1672	—EPRO S. P. 29/329 f. 33—	110
21.	————————	—October 7, 1672	—EPRO S. P. 29/329 f. 94—	111
22.	Pepys to Evelyn	—January 15, 1673	—PL Letters to Admiralty III, 37—	112
23.	————————	—January 24, 1673	—PL Letters to Admiralty III, 55–56—	113
24.	————————	—August 9, 1673	—PL Letters to Admiralty III, 98—	114
25.	————————	—October 7, 1673	—PL Letters to Admiralty III, 118—	114
26.	————————	—October 15, 1673	—PL Letters to Admiralty III, 225—	115
27.	Evelyn to Pepys	—January 30, 1680	—HL—	115
28.	Pepys to Evelyn	—January 31, 1680	—BL Rawlinson A 194, f. 135—	118
29.	Evelyn to Pepys	—June 15, 1680	—PL Miscellanea, V, 53–54—	118
30.	————————	—June 25, 1680	—ML—	119
31.	Pepys to Evelyn	—July 7, 1680	—PL Miscellanea, V, 61–62—	120
32.	Evelyn to Pepys	—July 7, 1680	—PL Miscellanea V, 65–89—	121
33.	————————	—September 6, 1680	—PL Miscellanea V, 56–58—	136
34.	————————	—January 8, 1686	—HSP—	139
35.	————————	—no date	—R—	140
36.	Pepys to Evelyn	—April 1687	—HSP—	141
37.	Pepys to Evelyn	—February 15, 1695	—BM Stowe 747, f. 45—	142
38.	Hewer to Evelyn	—September 13, 1705	—BM Add. MS 15,949 f. 47—	142
39.	Jackson to Evelyn			
		—September 13, 1705	—BM Add. MS 15,949 f. 46—	143
40.	Evelyn to Jackson			
		—September 15, 1705	—BM Add. MS 15,949 f. 46—	144
41.	Evelyn to Hewer	—September 16, 1705	—BM Add. MS 15,949 f. 47—	144

NOTE: *In transcribing the following manuscript letters I have attempted to hold as closely as possible to the original, even to reproducing incorrect Latin and Greek, and inconsistent punctuation. I have, of course, omitted catch words at the end of pages, decorative dashes, and the various marks under superimposed letters. Where the manuscript is torn or blurred or the writing undecipherable, I have recorded the fact in a footnote.*

I.

Evelyn to Pepys

[Holograph]

Says-Court 23^d: S^{br}:-65

S^r,

There are divers miserably sick prisoners at Wollwich, especialy in this bearers Ship: If they could be conveyd downe to our Fly-boates before Gravesend; Our Chirurgeon there might looke after them; & they have also a Guard; but you know I am prohibited realiving any at Wollwich, even of our Owne men: They might be, I suppose, at Eryth; but how shall we (when recoverd) secure them from running away? At Gravesend we are forc'd to make stay of one of ye Flie-boats on purpose, for the numerous sick-prisoners wch we could not march wth their fellows to Leeds; therefore I beseech you order them by some meanes or other to be sent (viz, the sick onely) to those Vessels at Gravesend, where there will be care taken for them:

S^r, Since I saw you yesterday, comes notice to me that of the 5000 £, I was to touch by promise this Weeke from Wm Kingsland [1] by order of my L: Ashley, no lesse than 3000 £, of it is diverted for other purposes from Oxford: consider wth indignation, the misery, & confusion all will be in at Chatham, & Gravesend, where I was threatend to have ye sick all expos'd, if by Thursday next I do not send them 2000 £; & in what a condition o^r prisoners at Leeds, are like to be: If my L. of Albemarle (to whom I am now writing) do not this: I say helpe now by an highhand; dreadfull will be ye consequences, & I will leave you to consider, at whose doores, this dealing at Oxon is to be layd; I am almost in despair, & you will pardon the passion

of S^r, y^r most faithfull Ser^t:

J Evelyn:

---

[1] Reading doubtful.

APPENDIX

2.

Evelyn to Pepys

[Holograph]

Says-Court 29th: 7^{br}-65

S^r,

This being but an iteration of what was Orderd on Thursday, when we were wth his Grace, I cannot divine how it comes to be repeated; But being told it was brought hither by two Captaines (in my absence this day at Erith) who it seemes applyd themselves to my Ld: for the conveying of their Sick-men (and indeede I have no quarters nearer than those places his Grace mentions Graves-end & Chatham being full) I suppose it was written to pacifie their importunity, and quicken ye raising of the moneys to be assign'd me: There was a Copy of the lett^r, left at my house wth it, which causes me to write thus confidently of the Contents: S^r, I am

Y^r most humble
& obedient Ser^t:
J Evelyn

The bearer hereoff (one of o^r Chyrurgeons) whom I sent to see the state of our sick, will give you an accoñt of the extreamist misery of both our owne & prisoners, for want of bread to prevent them from perishing

3.

Evelyn to Pepys

[Holograph]

Says-Court: 30th: S^{br}: 65

S^r,

The inclos'd had kiss'd y^r hands before this, had not the most infinite troubles of other dispatches in order to y^r Cōmands, hindered me and the present necessities of sending Orders to Woolwich & to places adjacent, for the Quartring of more Sick-men obtruded on us, but refused to be entertaind: I have sent for a Marshall to Chel[sea] [1] to send downe to Erith, & thence to Graves-end for Guards for ye prisoners, but I have not yet of him; nor can I heare of Assistants that will undertake to gouverne that affaire, if he fails me from London; One of my men, this afternoone, desiring to be dismissd in regard of ye Contagion: I inclose you the lett^r: you desird, and you must forgive the dissorderly writing, There is plainesse; truth in the particulars, & I am not solicitous of any mans censure of the forme, when I discharge my Conscience I know I shall be thought impertinent, unlesse you back me wth y^r attestations, & that w^h some zeale, w^h therefore I humbly supplicate of you: In the interim, I hope you not to look on me as sluggish in my station, or indiligent as far as my talent reaches; nor of so slauish & disingenuous a nature to be tyd to impossibility & servitude: I cannot do miracles, nor know I how to sell goods & treate wth the Merchant; but I can dispose such effects as shall be put into my hands for the discharge of w^t is intrustd to me, & if I should pretend to other excellencies, it were to abuse you; But I am at all moments ready (in accknowledgmete of these deficiencys,) to resigne the hono^r his Matie has don me, to greate [   ]:[1] I beseech you inter [   ][2] this to regard advantage, who am

      S^r,
        Y^r most obedient Ser^t:
          J Evelyn

X^{ck} at night
 I have not eaten one bit of
 bread to-day.
 Be pleasd to seale y^{rs} when perusd;
Look on Sr Wm Doolye last:
[   ][3]

---

[1] MS. torn.
[2] MS. blurred.
[3] Line blurred.

APPENDIX

4.

Evelyn to Pepys

[Holograph]

Says-Court 3:Octo^r-65

S^r,

I was in some doubt whither those Lett^{rs} you comanded me to prepare, ariv'd timely enough to accompany y^u to Court on Saturday-night; For finding divers Chyrurgeons, and Sick-persons at my dores who had come from Several places wth sad complaints that they could not procure quarters for them, I was forc'd to dispatch Warrants to ye Coñestables & other Officers to be ayding and assistant to my Deputyes, and some of these concernd me as far as Deale and Sandwich, where we are so overlayd, that they send them back upon us, and they perish in the returne; So that I had not a moments leasure to finish my letter, till it was neare 7 of ye Clock; and I would be glad to know whither my [   ]¹ came to y^r hande at all. S^r, I have had earnest intreaties from Severall of the Comanders (riding from Woolwich) to dispose of their Sick-& wounded-men on shore, but the Clearks of ye Cheg. there reproches o^r Chyrurgeon, and obstructs the effect of the Warrant I sent to ye Coñestable, upon a pretence, of bringing the Contagion amongst them; whiles in ye meane time, I am sure, they Suffer others to tipple in the Ale-houses; And Sr Theophilus Biddulph was wth me to spare Greenewich, because of y^r sitting there, and Deptford in reguard of his Maties Yard: I would be glad to know (Since Chatham, & Graves-End can hold no more) and that I have peopld all the intermedial Villages, what I shall do with those miserable Creatures, who are not able to move? Though had halfe of these but bread to eate (I speake not here of ye Prisoners, but o^r owne men) we should not have neere the multitudes, which are impos'd upon us. S^r, I do not tell you these stories out of any designe to engage or trouble you with other folkes businesse, as you have lately seem'd to impute it to me; because wthout monnye I could not feede two-thousand Prisoners; but to let you see, that it is not without reason I have made my Complaints nor at all my crime, if his Maties Subjects perish for want of harbor. It was

¹ MS. torn.

also presented[2] as a failure in my Industry, that I had not receiv'd the Prisoners into my [   ][3] and assisted towards the raising the 5000 £, to be assign'd me; But upon my [   ][3] applications to my Ld: Broneker & S^r Jo Mennes (according to his Graces direction) and my Yesterdays dispatching two very able Officers to take their names, receive them out of the respective prizes & shipps; there were none of these Vessells ready you were pleas'd to name, nor roome in them for a quarter of the number; so as my Martial return'd *re infactâ*, and could not fall downe wth them to Graves End when I had also provided Guards to secure them: For this Service S^r, I therefore yet attend y^r Comands, and am ready, when ye Vessels are so; and more then so, to take them quite off y^r hande, & the Vessels too when I have touch'd the mony which must make them live; having since I saw you contracted wth my Ld: Culpeper (fourty miles from this place) for Leeds-Castle, where I am repairing, & fitting things for their safty, that I may not seeme to be indiligent, because I am unhappy, & have no talent to rayse monnye, though I can tell where it may be had, when I know the Comodity: S^r, I have at this moment [4] Chelsey College, two Hospitals in Lond: & Nine other townes, besides Villages, where I have Deputys, Physitians, Chyrurgeons, & Martials, who employ me wth businesse sufficient to take up any one persons time, but to reply to their Lett^s: make them Warrants, send them Medicaments, Mates, Monye, if I had not the importunity of a thousand Clamors at my dores w^h neither lets me rest day nor night: S^r, in a Word, I have studied my Comission, & the Instructions annex'd to them, and I hope shall be able to justifie every Article, though I cannot compare my force and abilities wth others: Nor did I in the least obtrude the importunity w^h I am sensible the Prisoners have been to you; but upon his Grace's certaine knowledge of o^r want of monye to feed them, & without any provocation of mine (more than w^t you heard of o^r poverty) he was pleased to Order what was so very necessary, and I have not I hope presum'd to any favour upon my owne Score; for I no where find, by my Comission, that I was to provide monye, but to dispense it when I had it, & to

[2] Reading doubtful.
[3] MS. torn.
[4] [Note in margin] wch belong to all 4 Comiss^{rs} & not to my care alone.

give a just account of its application w^h I am ready to do wth joy: Nor have I yet been wanting in giving notice to the Greate-Ones at Court, from post to post-day (long before this as having prospect sufficient of w^t is befallen us) in a style more zealous & peremptory, than perhaps becomes me; and as I continu'd to do this very morning in a lett^r I writ to my Ld: High Chancell^r wch I sent by Sr Rich: Browne; having alarm'd all the rest (not one excepted) with my continual representations of o^r miserys: And if (as I could tell you from a Person that best knowes in England) I should shew you from whence this neglect of us proceeds, it would not add a Cubite to y^r stature: Be assur'd Sir, from me, that I shall be most tender of adding to y^r trouble, (whose burthen I find is already so insupportable) and I hope I shall not be esteem'd remisse, when I also keepe within my owne Sphere. What has come collateraly on you (not through my fault) ought not be imputed to me: And I hope when you know me well (as I am greatly ambitious of that honour) you will find I have taken too exact a measure of y^r real merits, and personal Civilities to me, then to forfeite them by my impertinencies; as I beseech you to believe, that I have not in this paper exaggerated any thing of mine Owne Sufferings, to magnifie the poore Service I have hitherto don (as by little arts we are prone to do) but that you would looke on me as a plaine-Man, who desires to Serve his Matie (till he is pleas'd to release me) in the station I am assigned to the best of my abilities; and which I shall be sure to improve, if you still allow me a part of y^r Esteeme, who cannot eclipse the brightnesse of y^r Example from

      S^r,
    Y^r most faithfull, and
     most obedient Servant
      J Evelyn

5.

Evelyn to Pepys

[Holograph]

Says-Court 13: Oct^r: 65

S^r,

I am this afternoone to send 1000£ to Deale and Dover wth a Guard, not having been able to find any opportunity of returning the mony otherwise; which will make me so unmannerly, as not to be able to waite on you as I ought: there is likewise another Calamity on me, from ye negligence of others; therefore (though the occasion be very instant, as to those Vessells for our pestiferous men) I must defer the kissing of y^r hands til to morrow, unlesse you resolve to do me the honor of refreshing y^r Selfe in our poore Garden any time this evening when you have best leasure, where I shall be to receive y^r Comands, who am

S^r
    Y^r most obedient
& faithfull Servant
    J Evelyn

6.

Evelyn to Pepys

[Holograph]

Says-Court 14th: O^{br}: 65

S^r,

By what I have sent you, you will have a Specimen of the Method observed where I have any-thing to do. If ye heads be not particular enough, be pleas'd to give me y^r instructions where I may pertinently add: Take notice also, I pray, how few have miscarried,[1] the last winter consider'd, notwithstanding our agreement at a certainety wch o^r D^{rs} & Chirurgeons 3£ [ ][2] head; to avoyd the unconscionable bills of ye Apothecaries, wch one article alone would have been double all the expenses, as by experience in the last Warr we learn'd:

---

[1] [Note in margin] Most of those who dyed perished for want of covering.
[2] per?

The Certificates answer to every individual person, which after you have perus'd, and are satisfied in, pray returne by this bearer; because they onely are my Vouchers; The other Accoumpt, keepe by you as long as y^u please; I having a duplicate; and call to us for the Whole when ever you please; because I long to give it in, & be discharg'd of so much of my Burthen: The two printed papers are an invention I have particularly practis'd in my owne Circle onely, wch I hope you will not reprove, because it dos a little obviate the querie of Sr Wm Coventry, to whom (if what I transmitt, prove satisfactory to you) speake your just thoughts of my Duty in the particular he mentions and add to y^r former favour, that of including these Lett^{rs} in y^r Packett for

S^r,
Y^r most obedient,
and faithfull Servant
J Evelyn

Mr Pepys etc.

7.

Evelyn to Pepys

[Holograph]

Says-Court 23^d: Oct^r: 1665

S^r,

Yours of the 17th Instant I found at my returne from Leades, and Kentish Circle, requiring an accoumpt of what Sea-men have been sick on shore? the ships whence they came? & the place to which? wth other p^{r}ticulars to encounter the fraud of y^r Purpose[1] etc S^r, for mine owne concerne, I sent you that of Deale, and am ready to p^{r}sent you with the rest of mine to the 5th of June last; since which we have not yet altogether finished the last quarter; but I presume may be ready with it to a day, by that time you have examin'd those: for those of my other Breathren, I presume they are also prepard for you: But I can give no positive account of it, they being all of them many miles distant from our place of meeting: In ye meane time

---

[1] Reading doubtful.

I have sent y^r Lett^r to Sr Wm Doily, that he may know w^t y^r Comands are: I verily believe his are in very good order, having lent him my Clearke so long, though to mine owne prejudice: With what concernes my Selfe as to this particular, I shall to morrow (God willing) waite on you, who am

    S^r,
     Y^r most obed^t
     & humble Servt
     J Evelyn

8.

Evelyn to Pepys

[Holograph]

[November 4, 1665]

I have six or seaven men who have spent us a greate deale of mony, & care at *Deale,* who are likely never to be cured, having some of them been dissmembrd, others dissabld by ulcerate sores of inveterate malignity, totaly unfit for any service: I once made it my suite to you (and y^u seemd to consent) that such persons might be discharg'd: be pleas'd to signifie what my Deputy, & Chirurgen (who are both ready to certifie this) shall do with them to

    S^r,
     Y^r
    most obedient Ser^t:
Says-Court   J Evelyn
4th: 9^br-65

9.

Evelyn to Pepys

[Holograph]

[November 23, 1665]

S^r,

 I am but just now ariv'd; of w^h I will give you no farther account at p^rsent, because the post shall not goe without the direction you require, though it be not so p^rticular as I could wish it: The last I

receiv'd was from Mr Fillingham, and since that he is gon very sick home to his owne house to which I have no other addresse than by Mr Fillingham; so that the most expeditious will be to enclose Sr W^{ms} Lett^{re} in a paper to him with this superscription For Mr Fillingham at Mr Loverans's in Hadleigh
to be left at Stratford beyond Colchester
       Suffolk:
S^r
Mr Conny (who is wth me) informes me of the indispensable necessity of having an Hospital Ship, & therefore conjures me to put you in mind of ye favour: Pardon dear S^r, this abrupt Scribble of
     S^r,
    Y^r most humble Ser^t
     J Evelyn

Says-Court at
7 the Clock.

10.

Evelyn to Pepys

[Holograph]

       Says-Court 7th: D^r-65

S^r,
 Forgive me that I beg the favour of having these Lett^{rs} convey'd to ye Post by your Ordinary Messenger this Evening: And that I do not let slip this opportunity of bespeaking y^r assistance and advice where I am to apply myselfe, that some effectual Course be taken with divers miserable Creatures under o^r Chirurg^{ns} hands (at Deale especially) to furnish them wth Clothes, that so they may at last be sent on board; since it is not health, but Covering which they have long wanted; and whilst they suffer this Calamity, spend his Matie five times the value in quarters: There are likewise more then 50, who being Old-Men, tabid, inveteratly Ulcer'd and universaly infirme, will never be render'd Serviceable to his Matie but have layne at prodigious expenses for Cure: As many as I have been able to convey, I have removed into ye Lond: Hospitals (since the abating of the Contagion amongst them has again opned their doores) but

some that are remote I cannot stir (for you have never allow'd us any boates to call as we beggd you would, & w^h would have aboundantly borne the charge of it) unlesse I should cart them: This I the rather mention because I have been frequently not onely promis'd they should have their Ticketts, & be lately discharg'd; but been injoyd to signifie their names to you: w^h both my Deputys and Chirurgions have don, with all necessary attestation: Yet still they remaine upon our hands: S^r, I depend very much upon y^r addresse in representing how much his Matie suffers by those two Inconveniences, whilst I can but give notice of them according to my duty, and as they occurr to

S^r,
    Y^r
      most humble &
      faithfull Servant
Mr Pepys   J Evelyn:

11.

Evelyn to Pepys

[Holograph]

Says-Court 9th Dec^r-65

S^r,

 Y^r Lett^r of the 7th concerning o^r Prisoners in the Golden-hand and Pr. Wi^lem came not an houre since to me; by what neglect I know not: I have sent to my Martiall at Leeds, to be here on Moneday (if possible) and to march away with them; so that those Vessells shall speedily be cleared: Sr Wm Coventry gives me hopes our Lazers shall be clothed, but you must coöperate or we shall be forgotten: I am S^r, *stylo Laconico*

    Y^r most faithfull Servant
      J Evelyn:
Mr Pepys

APPENDIX

12.

Pepys to Evelyn

[Copy signed by Pepys]

[December 12, 1665]

S^r

His Royal Highness hath comanded, that ye Golden hand & Prince W^m be imediatly sent to New Castle to fetch Coales for ye poore of ye Citty of London: I doe therefore entreat you that if they have any Dutch prisoners now onboard them as I am told they have that you will please to thinke of some fitt place for ye removal of them unto, & to cleare ye shipps of them [1] that we may in obedience to his Royal Highness's comands see ye said shipps imediately proceed on ye forenamed service: I am

Your affectionat Servant

S Pepys

Navy Office Greenw^{ch}
12, December 1665

13.

Evelyn to Pepys

[Holograph]

Says-Court 13th D^r-65

S^r,

Being now willing to remove not onely the Prisoners out of the Golden-hand and Pr Willm (according to y^r Comand) but likewise to Cleere all the Shipps at once that so you may be at full liberty for the future to dispose of them: I must humbly make it my request that you will facilitate the Worke by gratifing my Martial with y^r Warrant, impowering him to presse some tiltboate or other, as there shall be occasion, for the transporting them to Gravesend,

---

[1] Reading doubtful.

in order to their march: This, S^r, if you shall do, you will much oblige

S^r,
Y^r
most humble Servant
J Evelyn

My Martials name is M^r Jo Roawlandson
   Mar^{11} at Leeds-Castle
      Kent
Be pleas'd to send the Order to me by the Bearer himself.

14.

Evelyn to Pepys

[Holograph]

Says-Court Jan: 31:-65/6

S^r,

   I do, according to y^r Comands, transfer it you an hasty Draught of the Infirmary, and Project for Chatham; the reasons, and advantages of it, which challenges y^r promise of promoting it to the Use design'd: I am, my Selfe, convinc'd of the exceeding benefit it will every way afford us: If, upon examination of ye particulars, and your intercession, it shall merit a recomendation from the rest of the Pr^{ll} Officers, I am very confident the effects will be fully answerable to the pretence of the Papers which I send to accompany it: In all Events, I have don my Endeavor; and, if upon what appears ever Demonstrable to me (not without some considerable Experience, and frequent Conference wth o^r Officers, discreete, and sober Persons) I persist in my fondnesse to it, from a prospect of the many advantages would be reaped by setting it on foote; I beseech you to pardon the honest intentions, and to passe-by the Errors of

S^r,
Y^r
most obedient
and faithfull Servant
J Evelyn:

S^r, I must beg y^r excuse, if my desire to comply wth y^r comands as soone as might be, and having severall avocations, I could not delineate the Plot so accurately as I intended; but I hope it may suffice to explaine the Designe: neither had I one to write so fairely, as the paper inclosd in the rolle should have ben written:

Sam^{ll}: Pepys Esqr

15.

Evelyn to Pepys

[Holograph]

Says-Court 17: Feb: 65/6

S^r,

His Matie was well pleas'd wth what I shew'd him of o^r Infirmary for Chatham, which he gave me leave to explaine to him at large: If you have thought it worthy y^r recomendation to his Royal Hi^{sse} I would be glad to heare of the successe; being still as assur'd of its effects to all the purposes I pretend in the annexed papers, as ever: It were tyme something were resolv'd on before the Spring advance upon us, that we may apply it to the designe of

S^r,

Y^r most affect^t and
humble Servant
J Evelyn:

S^m Pepys: Esqr

16.

Evelyn to Pepys

[Holograph]

Sayes-Court 28: Feb: 65/6

S^r,

I had imediately yealded obedience to y^r Comands in going downe to Chatham, and prepard w^t was necessary to put that affaire in some forwardnesse, if I could have receiv'd the monyes which I have long expected that must enable me to appeare there; not for the carrying on of that Worke, but the discharge of our Sick-mens quarters there, my arreare being so greate, that I dare not shew my face, 'till I can bring them some refreshment: but so soone as I shall be enabld (and I am daily promisd monye) to appeare amongst them, I shall not retard my journey a moment, and so soone as I have (wth the advise of Mr Comiss^r Pett) made choyse of a fitting place; I shall either waite on you with the account of it, or transfer the p^{r}ticulars to you, if I find it necessary that my aboade there may more conduce to y^r Service: S^r, I beseech you be pleas'd to make part of this to the rest of the Prip^{ll} Officers from

     S^r,
      Y^r
       most humble
       & faithfull Servant
        J Evelyn:

Mr Pepys:

17.

Evelyn to Pepys

[Holograph]

         White-hall 16 Mar: 65/6

S^r,

 That I may by degrees observe y^r Comands, I do by this Bearer send you the Dover Accp^t for ye p^{r}sent occasion, and the rest as fast as they are return'd me; this day & every day expecting those of Deale & Gravesend etc: Be pleasd to returne me by this hand, the P^{r}ticulars, on hand of ye estimate I gave you of our proposd Infirmary, that it may direct me to draw up & calculate what I am to laye before you upon this expedition to Chatham wch I shall do, so soone as I have an houre to spare from my p^{r}sent miseries &

learne¹ how to get a little monye to relieve your sick flock in my district: I am S^r, wth all affection

      Y^r
      most humble
     & obedient Servant
       J Evelyn:

S^r,

Since the writing hereof, I have certaine tidings of our Deale Accpt: & am promisd it shall be given you in tomorrow.

18.

Evelyn to Pepys

[Copy]

[August 21, 1669]

If you make yor Journey through Picardy (wch I believe you may resolve to do in regard to ye Contagion) if you could so contrive it as to see Monsr de Lion-Court's Seat at Lion-Court, the Gardens & Water-works would much please you; at least, if they are continu'd with that Care we have knowne them. But because I cannot tell how inconvenient it may prove to deviate so far from yor direct Road, I do only mention it en passant.

Calais you will find a Strong Town by ye new Fortifications & by two adjoining Forts, besides ye Citadelle & ye Sluces, by wch they can environ it with Water at pleasure. The Market-place & Magazine, wch was once a Staple for English Wool is observable; & so is ye Architecture of an Altar-piece (as I take it) of black marble. I us'd to lodge at ye Silver Lyon. Hence you have 7 Leagues to Boulogne a small Town; but famous for our H. 8's Expedition. The Lower Town has a large Street, & there I suppose you may lodge au Bras d'or. The Fortifications are not considerable. After 7 Leagues riding you will come to Montreuil, where you will see an irregular Citadel; but ye Town situated on a Strong Eminence; and towards

¹ Reading doubtful.

Paris-side ye Fortification is very considerable by an Horn-work, & most noble Bastions, which are worth Remark, & will give you an Idea of ye Strength of such Places as they fortify abroad.

Abbeville is 10 Leagues, a reasonable pretty Town; and thô it be well fortify'd, there is nothing very observable in it. Here they use to offer us Pistols & Guns to buy. I think you will lodge there, or proceed 4 Leag. further to Pont Dormis. A Little Strong Place regularly fortify'd. Thence to Crevecoeur 4 Leagues: And thence to Poix Where you come into wretched Places, till you arrive at Beauvais 9 Leag. (as I remember) a pretty large Town, & Market-place, & well water'd: The Houses built of Wood. The Bishop's House is of Stone, & has some good Appartments in it. The Church is imperfect; but ye Architecture good, though plain, & with handsome Sculpture behind ye Quire. Pray observe the Measures of ye Town for their Serges, & ye Standards of them by Iron Chains of different Lengths. After 8 Leag. you come to Beaumont.

Here, & before you will enter among ye Vine-yards, I know little more observable, except it be ye House & Garden of ye President Nicolais, as you draw near Paris; which I esteem much for ye Avenue & Fountains. But your mind will be so set on Paris, wch is now but 4 leag. distant, that you will hardly stay. And indeed this whole Journey will render you little satisfaction, being for ye most part, through a Frontier and miserable Country, and where you will see part of ye Calamity of a Tyrannical Government, & ye Effects of a continual War, such as has afflicted all that Tract for diverse Years. When you are arrived at Paris, my Counsel is, that you take Chambre garnie (as they call it) Sr Saml Tukes addresses you to a Friend of his, an Irish Doctor of Physick (unknown to me) who he assures me will be so honest, humble, & necessary to you, that you shall need no other to conduct you to all ye considerable Places, and to introduce you both at ye Courts & oth^r Assemblys, which it is necessary for you to see. He will likewise find you out a convenient place for yor Lodging, and do ye Offices of a Guide in all that you can desire; and which will therefore much shorten ye trouble I was going to engage you in, by giving you any large Directions of my owne—

That yet, this Paper may serve to put you in mind of some Particulars, wch happly ye Shortness of yor Expedition may otherwise indanger you to omit. I would in ye first place climb-up into S. Jacques Steeple to take a Synoptical Prospect of that monstrous City, to consider ye Situation, Extent, & Approaches; so as to be ye better able to make Comparisons with our London; which you will do with pleasure, by imagining it extended to a Length which you will find in a Circle.

The principal Places where Persons of Quality dwell are in ye Suburbs, especially that of St Germains, & in that ye Abbey, an old Foundation, but nothing much remarkable in it. But ye Hospital of la Charité is worthy yor seeing, for ye worthy Charity wch is every day there exercis'd in so full, so cleanly & devout a manner, as must needs much affect you; especially when you shall have seen ye rest of those admirable Foundations, among wch you must not forget ye Hostel-Dieu near Notre-Dame, though it be not altogether so neat and compt; yet by ye Number & manner of it, very considerable.

There are diverse noble Houses in these Fauxbourgs; but none comparable to that of

Luxembourg call'd le Palais d'Orleans; wch for ye Fabrick & Garden (now I hear much neglected since ye Decease of ye best Gardiner in ye World, the Duke) is exceedingly worthy yor frequent Visite. Consider ye Building well, and ye Extent of ye Ground about it, as within so great a City; The Fountains, Walks, Eminency on wch it stands; and you will judge it almost as fine as Clarendon-House, whose Situation somewhat resembles it. The Duke's Library & Gallery well furnish'd with Books, and incomparable Medals (of which he was ye most knowing and curious Person in Europ) together with ye Gallery painted by ye Hand of Rubens (so as we have none in England, and therefore our Painters know not what belongs to Historical Works) will exceedingly please You, if these Curiosities remain still in ye Lustre they did at my Sojourn there.

In ye City, the first Place of Note is ye Louvre, or Court of that Great Monarch. The Gallerie, Salle of Antiquities, Printing-house, Monnoye, Gardens of ye Thuilleries, Furniture, Architecture, & ten thousand Particulars will take you up a good time here. Besides that you ought to kiss the K. & Q.'s Hands; to see some publick

Audience; observe his Table, his Guard, Council, & what else will be suggested to you by yor Conductor. As you go to Court, you will pass over Pont-neuf, and wish ours of London had no more Houses upon it, but instead thereof a Statue, such as you will there find erected, the Work of ye famous Giovanni de Bologna, greatly esteem'd. At ye foot of this Bridge (for ye River is not considerable) there was a Water-work call'd ye Samaritaine, & in my time such a curious and rich Piece of Artificial Rock-Work, as was hardly to be seen in Europ. But ye curious Person that then was Master of it, is since many years dead, & perhaps ye Rock demolish'd and sold: It is but asking ye Question. However one would see ye Machine.

Notre-Dame is ye Chief Church of Paris, built (as Tradition goes) by ye English, but infinitely inferiour to St Pauls, or Westminster. You will do well to consider it; if ye Giant at ye Entry do not forbid you. There are some Pictures in it considerable.

Near this is ye Pont au Change, which though but short, is for ye uniformity of ye Houses & Bass-relieve of Brass at ye front of it, pretty in perspective.

You will be much entertain'd in visiting ye several Convents of ye Orders of Fryers & other Religious Men: One would therefore see ye Convents of ye Franciscans, Capucines, Fathers of the Oratory, and above all ye Jesuites, both that of the Novitiate in ye Suburbs near Luxembourg, for ye trueness of ye Architecture, & though plain, yet very excellent and that of St Louis, more splendid & costly. And you must not only behold ye Out-side, but procure Admission within to see their manner of living, which will bee wholly new to You; especially that of ye Carthusians, wch I conjure you not to omit; & to visit likewise a Nunnery or two, not forgetting Lion, and ye Monument of Sr Saml Tukes's Lady.

When among ye sever^l Churches & Oratories you shall have once well contemplated ye Val de Grace, yor Eyes will never desire to behold a more accomplished Piece. There it is you will see ye utmost effects of good Architecture & Painting, & heartily wish such another stood where once St Pauls was, ye boast of our Metropolis; for than this, you will never see a more noble (though not great Fabrick;) the Convent and other Buildings about it are very compleat, especially the Carmes over against it.

After ye Churches & Hospitals, remember ye University, particularly the Sorbonne. The Schools are a plain Building, but ye Church is a noble Structure, & ye melancholy Situation of it within ye Court, has some what (methinks) of particular in it, which affects me. Here, be sure to be at some publick Scholastical Exercise, & love our owne Universitys ye better after it.

There is le College des quatre Langues founded by C. Mazarin, but not yet finish'd, worthy your Enquiry after. And if his Ma^ty have done any thing for ye Virtuosi (our Emulators) in designing them a Mathematical College, seek after it, & procure to be admitted into their present Assembly, that you may render our Society an Account of their Proceeding. You will easily obtain that by ye assistance of some Friend: But Mr Oldenburg being in ye Country, (for I went to his House) you will miss of an infallible Adress.

Now you must be sure to be early at some famous Academy to see ye Gent. ride ye Great Horse, & their other Exercises, that you may be astonish'd a great Kingdom as ours, & so great a City as London, should not afford one Cavalerizio for ye noblest Institution of Youth; there being so many in Paris, & in almost all ye considerable Citys of France, wch daily ride near an hundred managed Horses.

When you visit le Palais Cardinal, You will find many things worth yor seeing, especially ye Galeries and the Painting; the K. & Q.'s Bathing-Rooms, Chambers of Audience; Theater for ye Comedies, Gardens, and near it Card. Mazarin's Palace, at my being in Paris, & in his Life-time, doubtless ye most richly furnish'd in the World.

I suppose ye Library is yet extant: You must by all means see it, as one of ye most considerable things in Paris.* But what is of greater Antiquity, & to be reverenc'd for being so, is, the Abbey de St Victoire whose Bibliotheq is very remarkable. But infinite are the Collections of rare Books, Pictures, Statues, Curiositys, &c., which ye Noblemen & many private Persons have in Paris; which daily augmenting & diminishing, according to ye genius of ye Possessors of them, You must enquire after upon ye Place, & procure means of seeing: For wch I transmit you the 3 Enclos'd Letters to Friends of mine (though of ye lower Rank) who will abundantly

* But ye King has a Library well worth yor seeing near Monsr Colbert's house.

satisfy yor Curiosity; and you will do well to purchase of them what they have of most rare of their own Works, as well Books as Tailles-Douces; the One being ye most famous Artist for things in Graving with ye Burin, & ye other in Etching. Monsr Du Bosse's Books of Architecture & Perspective etc. are worthy yor Collections. And if you stayd so long to have yor Lady's & yor own Pictures engraven by le Chevalier de Nanteuille you would bring home Jewels not to be parallel'd by any Mortal at present, & perhaps by none hereafter. He is ye greatest Man that ever handled ye Graver, and besides, he is a Scholar and a well-bred Person. And Monsr Du Bosse (ye other) is a plain, honest, worthy, & intelligent good man; both my Singular Friends & Correspondents for those Matters of Art etc.

The King's Medicinal Garden & Laboratory with all y^t Apparatus, is at no hand to be omitted, because it is so well furnish'd and so rarely fitted for ye Design, as having all ye affections of Ground & Situation desirable. If you stayd a whole Winter in Paris, I would invite you to see a Course of Chimistry, which is both there & in several private Places shew'd to ye Curious to their wonderful satisfaction and Benefit of Philosophic Spirits. Near to this is the Gobelins, where was wont to be ye Manufacture of Tapestry; pray enquire it out most diligently, and by no means omit ye visiting of all those Particulars, no, not Monsr Colbert's late Silk-Worm-Work, or whatever there be of that Nature.*

You must likewise see ye Hostel de Ville, being their Guild Hall, ye Palais (which is their Exchange) & there the Hall of Justice; answerable to ours of Westminster, neater, but not so large, especially the Parliament-Chamber & other Tribunals, which you will find to be much more august & splendid than most of ours. Here you will take notice of ye Habits of their Advocates & Men at Law, & be curious to hear a Pleading, as well as a Masse & other Ceremonies at some of the Churches, that you may love yor own Religion ye better.

The Place Royal is our Piazza of Covent-Garden; but in my judgment nothing so chearful. The Brazen Horse in it is considerable.

By some especial Favour you may be admitted to take a View of

* At these Gobelins are all ye K's Manufactures: Pray therefore visit it most studiously.

ye Bastille (which is their Tower) and Arsenal joyning to it. There you will see in what Equipage for Strength they are; for there they cast their great Guns, and there is ye Repository of Stores. There are many noble Houses and pretty Oratories here-about, especially St Louis belonging to ye Jesuites, with a Noble Frontispice.

For once you would be at ye Preach at Charenton, & for once see a publick Comedy at l'Hostel de Bourgogne, and even ye Madmen at ye Petites-Maisons: For all these Places & Humours are instructive; but none more divertissant than the Mountebanks and prodigious Concourse of Mankind au Pont Neuf, wch I would therefore have you frequently to traverse, & contemplate, as a lively Image of that Mercurial Nation.

In ye St Chappel are some Reliques wch you may also see, when you are at ye Palais; & be sure to bring home with you some good French Books, wch you will encounter in your visiting their Shops.

The Cours you should likewise see, to compare it with our Assemblys of Gallants & Faire Ladys at Hide-Park: And then I know not what to say more; for by this time you will be willing to take some air perhaps abroad, & make a Journey about ye Town, to see how they live in ye Countrey, & how they make their Wine (for ye Vintage almost meets you) among their Villa's. The Places I recommend to yor view are chiefly,

St Cloud, those Noble Gardens, where you will kiss ye Hand of Madame la Duchesse d'Orleans. Ruel, formerly a most elegant Villa St Germain en Laye, one of ye K's Countrey-Houses, nobly situated, & where there were the most Artificial Water-Works & Grotts in France, now I hear run exceedingly to decay. Maisons in my poor Judgment for ye Architecture, Situation, Cutt into ye River, Forest, Gardens, Stables &c. one of ye most accomplish'd & sweet Abodes that ever I saw: But it is not perfect. Madrid is not very considerable; but one Appartment at Bois St Vincennes is worth yor view, with ye Park; of wch you will find none comparable to ours in England. St Denys, I suppose, you might see in yor Journey going or returning; and there, besides a venerable Church, ye Dormitory of ye French Kings, a Treasury of Reliques emulating even that of our Lady's of Lorette, and you must not omit it.

I would have you also make a step to Arcueil, which Mary of

Medicis built for an Aquaeduct; because it will furnish you with an Idea what those Stupendious Structures were extended to many miles, and of greater Altitude only.

Chantilly, Melun, Verneuil, Monceaux, Villers Cotteret, Limours, Bois le Vicomte, Bisestre, an Hospital, are Countrey-Palaces and Gardens of great Fame, if yor time serve you may do well to visit.* But at no hand must you forget to take a through Survey of their renowned Fontainebleau; which when you have seen you will not judge comparable to Hampton-Court; nor can ye French Monarch shew such a Castle, Palace, & Church, as our Windsor in all his wide Dominions. Yet here ye Canal, & plenty of Water, with ye Forest about it is stupendious; and there are some good Paintings in ye House; but especially that Gallery, ye Work of ye famous Prima Titia.

Versailles will much please you; & Veau, the House of ye late President Fouguet, amaze you for ye infinite Cost both in Building & Gardens, august even in its very Ruins, & absence of its magnificent Founder.

I had forgott to acquaint you that ye Church-yard of St Innocents in Paris is observable for ye Quality of ye Earth, wch by ye innumerable Buryings there, is become Sarcophagus; & there it is you will see ye Hieroglyphics of ye Philosophic Works of Nic. Flamel; but in nothing beautifull or considerable.

I should not have so slightly mention'd les Carmes, a Church near Val de Grace, because it is most worthy yor seeing, and particularly ye Tabernacles upon ye High Altar.

In ye English Coll. of Jesuites, Clermont, you will see ye Systems of Copernicus, and ye new Astronomers, moved by Water; For ye rest, the place is nothing observable.

S^r, Had I anything more to add, I should weary you; it is already late, & I almost blind: So as I am perfectly asham'd at my wretched Character.

J E

* Many of those Places will be too far for you.

19.

Evelyn to Pepys

[Holograph]

Rochester 27 Aug:-72
10 at night:

S^r,

I suppose you have ben told of a greate deale of noise that was made at Gravesend when the Comiss^{rs} (your Colleagues) pass'd by: But they could not informe you, how difficult a thing it will allwayes be, to quarter 800 people in a towne that can hold but 500, and where we had neere 200 before: But this is the condition of Gravesend, and Mr Pearse the Chirurgion Gen^{rl} had advertisement of it: I came hither one Sunday, and found not a man but was decently quarterd, or provided for; nor has there ben dead above 5 of all this number, whereof 2 were brought dead out of ye Vessell, & maliciously exposd in the Streete to improve the Clamor, which will never be appeas'd till monye be sent, to discharge the awards, notwithstanding that I have engagd my selfe for no inconsiderable sum: I have ben visiting Chacham, Rochester, & the Fleete & put all things in perfect order, save my selfe who have never ben in bed since Saturday last: But when all imaginable care is taken, as to our part, unless you be pleasd to allow some Covering to the poore Creatures, who are (many of them) put stark naked & mortified, on the shore: multitudes of them must perish; and therefore (presuming on y^r Charity, & indeede humanity) I have adventur'd to give way, that some of the most miserable should have shirts or stockings (according to their needes) to preserve them from perishing; and I do by those, beg of you, to Order y^r Shope Tellers to send a Competent number of such necessaries to our Deputies at Gravesend & Rochester: or to any other Person, whom you shall think fit to trust: That his Mat^{ie} may not loose his Subjects for want of so slight, and yet necessary supply: I do assure you Sr This is a very material thing, & therefore I do againe implore you to take it to heart: We have neere 2200 sick people in quarters in this province, amongst which divers are sadly ulcerated for want of cloathes & charge: Such as are in any tollerable Condition, a few daies will perfect, though at present every tide increases the numbers: But those cursed people of Gravesend have no bowels and sweare they will receive not a man more, till their arears are discharg'd: We are above 2000$^£$ indebted in Kent, where our daily charge is 100$^£$ p^r diem for quarters onely; Judge by this how comfortable a station I am in, & whither all this clamor, has ben comparable to the occasions of the poore Inhabitants who give us Credit: But enough of this, from S^r

    Y^r most humble &
    faithfull Servant
     J Evelyn

I beseech y^u remember ye Sleepe etc:

20.

Evelyn to Pepys

[Holograph]

       Star-Chamb^r:
       20th: Sep^r:-72.

S^r,

 The Lett^r directed by y^r Board to the Comiss^{rs} for Sick & Wounded, I shall take care to comunicate to all my absent Breathren; and have in the meane time, sent it to the severall Ports; and Places within my precincts, with expresse Orders to o^r Officers that they do imediately set upon the Worke, and transmitt to you the Effects of their dilligence with all expedition, beginning with those ships specified in the margent: There is no question but there will be many found to have faild of their duty in returning to the Fleete, not withstanding all the law which could be apply'd to prevent it; and that it will cost some time to methodize the Lists as you are pleas'd to direct, but it shall be hastened with all y^e speede which may be from

$\qquad$ S^r,
$\qquad\qquad$ Y^r
$\qquad\qquad\qquad$ most humble &
$\qquad\qquad\qquad$ faithfull Servant
$\qquad\qquad\qquad\qquad$ J Evelyn

21.

Evelyn to Pepys

[Holograph]

$\qquad\qquad\qquad\qquad\qquad\qquad$ Star-Chamb^r 7/8^{br}-72

S^r,

$\quad$ I received the lett^r which was your reiterated exception, that the lists transmitted to y^r board from severall of our districts were not subscrib'd by the respective Deputies: In your first Instructions to us, that particular was not (as I remember), mentiond; and as soone as you were pleasd to renewe y^r directions, I tooke care that the Officers within my Circle should not omitt it: It is true, they have not as yet, all of them, dispatch'd what you desire: but it has not ben for want of all imaginable incitement, & which I have againe renew'd: You may please to call to mind, that you rejected that of Chatham & Feversham (which were the most considerable in my Circle) upon account of another omission, which they are now rectifying, and I do every moment expect it, together with that of Gravesend: In the meane time, as to those which came lately to you from Sr Wm Doylies District, I am very well assur'd that they are Authentiq, being accompanied with the Letters of his Agents in those parts, whose hands we are acquainted withal; If your Comands be positive, that I should returne them back againe for their Subscription onely, It will require time; but if you shall be pleas'd to dispence with that omission, (upon my presumption that Sr Willm Doyly dos owne them) there neede be no interruption in y^r proceeding to pay off the men: In all events, I am writing to Sr William, and shall advertise

him of it—S^r, I am oblig'd to write to you in the singular number, there being onely my selfe in Towne of the rest of my Collegues, to my very greate trouble: I had else made a journey my selfe to have set all this right in my quarters long before this time; and my Solicitude for monye (being indebted at Chatham alone neare 4000$^£$ besides w^t is owing in five or six other places) keepes me in perpetual drudgery: But, I hope you will receive all Satisfaction as to what you require about the Lists in a very few dayes. I remaine
    S^r,
        Y^r most humble Servant
        J Evelyn:

22.

Pepys to Evelyn

[Copy]

                Derby House 15th Jany. 1673.
S^r.

I have lately rec^d a letter from one of the Officers of the Duke of Albermarle's Regiment from Dover, wherein he acquaints me that Severall of the Souldiers of that Regiment Shipped on board the Marygold in the Downes, was sicke so that they were necessitated to putt them on Shore, and that there being no order for providing for them, yor Agent att Dover had att ye instance of the Officers taken care for sending them up to convenient quarters. But in regard he had no directions therein from the Com^{rs} for Sick and wounded Seamen, he did desire y^t the same orders might be given concerning those Sould^{rs} in the Marygold, as was for those in the Blessing for the indempnifying yor: Agent in what he has done. Whereupon I have procured the like order from his Maty in this Case as was in the former, and send the same to y^u enclosed. Remaining
        S^r: Yo^r very humble Servant.
           S. P.
M^r: Evelyn.

23.

Pepys to Evelyn

[Copy]

Jany: 24 [1673?]

S^r

Before I durst thinke itt fitt for me to write anything to Deale to ye Effect y^u desired I thought it expedient to satisfy my selfe from my Brother as particularly as I could whether the refractoriness of the Persons he Complaines of might not arise either from the pressure of the Arrears due to them for Charges past, or apprehension (by ye example of their neighbours) of the uncertainty of their being better used for what is to come. And as I foresaw I doe find from him that this is ye ground of y^t unwillingness wth wh^{ch} ye poore people there doe receive any new Burthens by the putting upon them any fresh numbers of Sick men from ye Fleete, Which being so, and led thereto from ye reason of ye thing no less than from the Captiousness of the times wherein wee now are, I am of opinion, that itt is neither fitt with regard to ye Honour of his Ma^{tys} Service nor ye Safety of any of his Servants that anything like Severity or threats should bee used upon any of ye persons complained of without good advise and express order, either from his Ma^{ty} or those of his Ministers who are better able both to advise and justifie what shall be fitt to bee determined concerning them. Therefore lett me desire y^u not to expect or depend upon any single interposition from me in the matter; but consider whether itt may not bee more advisable, both with regard to yo^{r}self and the History of itt to ye King's Service, y^t y^u make a representation of ye matter to his Maty. or my Lord of ye Counsill and receive their directions for yor further proceedings. In wh^{ch} as farre as any Solicitation of mine can bee either usefull to the King, or gratefull to y^u y^u shall comand

Yo^r most affect humble Servt

S. P.

Jany: 23^d. Esqr: Evelin.

24.

Pepys to Evelyn

[Copy]

[August 9, 1673]

The Lords Com^{rs} of ye Admi^{lty} meeting to morrow morning at ye Robes Chamber, I am Com̄anded by y^{or} Lo'ps to desire you to attend them there about 9 of ye Clocke, remaining

Yo^r humble Servt
S P

W. hall-9 Aug. '73
Evelin Esqr

25.

Pepys to Evelyn

[Copy]

[October 7, 1673]

S^r.

This comes onely to acquaint you that his Matie haveing directed James Pierce Esq Chyeurg etc. to go down to ye Burgess's House in ord^{er} to ye informing him selfe of ye true state of the S. & wounded men on board ye Fleete, the Buck Dogge[1] appointed to attend ye businesse of S. & W: is appointed to carry downe to ye Fleete & bring up againe the Sd. Mr Pierce and there to be at yor dispose, In ye meanwhile it would not be amisse to send at present some well Men [who][2] are now ready to ye Fleete by her. I remain

Y^{or} most humble Servt
S P.

8th: 7: 73
Mr. Evelyn.

[1] Reading doubtful.
[2] Editor's suggestion.

26.

Pepys to Evelyn

[Copy]

Whitehall 15: Octobr: 73

S^r

This comes only to observe to you that both by the dayly List from ye Downes & by Those I have this day read from ye Command^r of ye Buck Dogg^e: it doth not appeare y^t you either have for some time past or are now designing to make any use of that vessell; If I am in an errour pray rectify me, if otherwise I shall desire you will let me know it that ye Vessell being at Liberty from your service, I may make it my care to see her either usefully employed on some other part of His Ma^{te} Service, or called in and discharged. I remaine

Your very humble Servt:

S P.

Mr Evelyn.

27.

Evelyn to Pepys

[Holograph]

[January 30, 1680]

S^r,

It has ben greatly my hopes, & continualy my Wishes, (from some little hints that I have observ'd sometimes to fall from you) that upon this Recesse especially, & calme from publiq businesse; furnish'd as you are with a noble Library; & instructed by the greatest experience, joyn'd to an Industrie & Capacity (beyond any Mortal man that I know) of undertaking so use-full & desir'd a Work; That from *You* the Learned and curious World, might one-day receive that hitherto conceil'd *Arcano del Mar,* with the most consumate perfection & advantage: Sure I am, there is no Subject more worthy your choice, more illustrious for dignitie, & more capacious for the exercising all the parts of Historical, Mathematical, Mechanical; yea, the Critical and politer Learning, than what Lies fairely within the

Circle of that Mysterie, and within your ample Sphere—*Macte ergo Vir Cl:* & give y^r Prince, y^r Country & y^r Friends a Treasure, which 'tis certaine you have improv'd, and owe, if not to the whole ungratefull World, yet to in-numerable in it, who love & honor you; and by a generosity becoming a better nature, diffuse that good amongst us.

As to Books, & Multitude of Authors, subsidiary to this Attempt; They may possibly serve others (as me they have, some few smatterers for incouragement & diversions) whilst You have at once but to Recollect y^r owne Experiences, & Methodize those rich Materials which I am confident you have prepar'd in aboundance, & dispos'd for such a structure: You were lately pleas'd to enquire of me, what Authors I knew that had treated on this Subject *Data operâ:* It were but to cast a Mite into your opulent stock, should I undertake to enumerate any you have not consulted: In a trifling *Essay* I cursorily made use of some notes, that in my Course of reading, I had transcrib'd into my *Adversaria;* but I cannot call to mind any of importance (antient or modern) after I have nam'd *Duke Dudly, Furniere, Marishons,* the Late *Architecture Navale* publish'd in French, & that Worke of de *Witesen* in the Belgic tongue; which I conceive to be the most perfect extant as to the purely Mechanic part: The Historical & Ornamental, which should give grace to the whole, are to be fetch'd from the Philologians, *Athenaeus, Plinie, Vegetius, Frontinus:* & you are not unacquainted with *Lazius, Baijfius, Czesentias, Meibonius,* our *Selden, Grotius;* nor the Fragments in the *Notitia Imperii,* the Learn'd *Bochartus, Simeon Admirandus,* his Laws & Ordinances of the Admiralty, *gli Navigatione di Nearcho,* & the various Tracts de *dominio Maris* to be found all together (as I remember) among the *MSS* of Mr Selden in ye publiq Library at Oxford: All the Greeke & Latine Historians contribute to this noble work; especially *Herodotus, Thycidides, Polybius, Diodorus, Livy, Justine, Pomponius, Mela, Plutarch, Strabo,* the French, Dutch & Spanish Navigations, above all, the English for such Adventures and Exploits as any way concerne the Sea etc: But the greate, & usefull part will be the *Mathematical* and *Mechanical,* both for ye structure & Government of these stupendious and goodly Machines, together with a *Rationale* of every particular that concernes a Royal

Navy, ships of War, & Onerary Vessels for Trading; Harbour, Moles, Docks, & Magazines, The Admiralty, & other Officers, with the universal Oeconomic belonging in any sort to this Mysterie; of all which you can certainly give the most usefull & distinct Accounts, with what improvements have ben made from all ages, downe to the present, & what are the desideratos wanting to its perfection. S^r, I wish with all my heart, I could be any ways capable of subserviency in this, or any thing else; I confess, in regard that providence has cast my Lot so neere to *Zabulon* & a Naval Station, I have often wish'd I had ben worthy some inferiour Employment, that might (by this time) have render'd me more fit to Serve you; but it has not ben my good fortune hitherto; and however you may have heard, that I am now a Candidate for some such thing in this Shuffling of the Cards; yet my prospect reaches (I assure you) no farther, than the good wishes of some Friends, who I have heard have mention'd me; but truely, with very slender concerne or importunity of my owne; thô I can see no reason why I should reject any honorable Employ, which I might fairly obtaine, without Envy or reproach; since as to the discharge of such a Trust, as every one had a beginning once; so 'tis possible, an extraordinary application & religious integrity, might perhaps supply the defects of profounder Science; And he that has given Hostages to Fortune, as I have don, cannot, I perswade my Selfe be reprov'd by so worthy a Friend, as I esteeme You to be; without whose Counsel & Assistance, I should never hope to Emerge in any Sort: This just Apologie I make to Encounter the Reports which Mr *Hewer* told me Yesterday went about, as if I aym'd at high matters, & things that I understand not: But of all this, with the frankest Offer of my humble Service in any Capacity within my narrow reach; I shall declare my Thoughts farther to you, when I may not importune you, and that you are at any Leisure to Sacrifice so much time to the Impertinences of
    S^r
      Y^r most humble &
      faithful Servant
          J Evelyn

White-hall
30: Jan: after Supper

28.

Pepys to Evelyn

[Holograph]

Jan^{ry} 31st 16 79/80

S^r

Much I ought, & much I would say to you, in answr to yor kind transport in yors of last night, & ye point more particularly relateing to yor selfe in ye Close; Wherein I would to God any Service or advice of mine may be usefull. But an attendance I am now bound upon into London, will not give leave presently to doe it. I shall nevertheless bee at full leisure after 4 oClocke to wayte on you, & will doe it where-ever you will appoint mee by a word directed to mee at My Ld Privy Seale's in Drury-Lane, where I am under an obligacōn of dineing to day in company wth Mr Povey. I am

Y^{or} most aff^t & obed Servt
S P.

Mr Evelyn

29.

Evelyn to Pepys

[Copy]

A Letter from Mr Evelyn to Mr Pepys, in general relation to Navall Matters

Says-Court
Deptford 15 June 1680

S^r:

It was not 'till Sunday last (for I had been almost an intire weeke before from home) that Mr Holden acquainted me you would be willing to know, where one might finde that History of the Navy, which in my Booke of Comerce I speake of as sett forth by Edwd 3^d I have as near as I could in soe cursorie a Trifle, obtruded nothing upon the Reader, but what I have Authority for, and therefore not to send you to ye Reports of suspected writters you may please at your

Leasure, to Consult ye Roll it selfe, as it was lately extant (and doubtless yett is) in y^e Acco^t of his Ma^{ts} Greate Wardrobe, whereof one Willm Nowells was y^e Keeper: The Accompt is from 21st Aprill in that Princes 18 yeare to y^e 29th of Novembr of his 21st, and for all those 700 ships 14151 Marin^{rs} the whole expense amounted not to above 337000$^£$: 9^s: 4^d: which is worthy observacōn, as alsoe that Yarmouth sett forth as many more Ships as any Port of England. There is not yett by 400 Vessells, soe Vast a Navy as you will finde this noble Prince to have equipp'd for another expedicōn, which consisted of Anno 1359 Undecies centum Naves, et cum hoc apparatu, ad humiliandum Francorū factum (to use my Authors owne words) Tho Walsingham in his History; but the other was for ye Seige of Callais, S^r I have noe more to add, but that if I were soe happy as to know wherein I might contribute to any thing wch might be of use to your more curious researches, you have ever at your Service

S^r Yo^r most devoted and humble Servt
J Evelyn.

30.

Evelyn to Pepys

[Holograph]

1680, June 25, Whitehall

S^r

I did not intend to have given you this interruption this morning, & therefore did not write any answer to your kind [   ]^1 forbidding me to trouble you this day, when you had so much better Company: but when y^r Servant was gon, reflecting on the Excuse you injoyne me to make to Sir Jos. Williamson this Evening, I could not forbeare to wish that (if it were possible) you would give one halfe-houre of your presence & assistance toward (as I think) the most material Concerne of a Society, which ought not to be dissolv'd for want of a redresse, which is yet certainly in its power; and I would not have it thought, that you therefore absent y^r selfe, because in giving a free Suffrage, it may possibly displease some-one

---

^{1} Word undeciphered.

in the Company, that will be brought to no tolerable termes: I do assure you we shall want some of y^r Courage & addresse to encourage & carry-on this affair: You know we do not usually fall on businesse 'til pretty late, in expectation of a fuller Company; & therefore, if you decently could fall in amongst us by 6 or 7, it would (I am sure) infinetely oblige not onely those who mete, but the whole Society.

As to ye Queries, they are of that Substance, as I were too imodest to pretend I should at any time (much lesse at present) be able to give you full satisfaction. But, so soone as I get home (wh I hope to do after I have kissed y^r hands to-morrow) and have a little time to rummage my slender Collections; I will endeavor to let you see how exceedingly I am dispos'd to promote any Comands which come from Mr Pepys to

S^r, this most humble Servant
J Evelyn

31.

Pepys to Evelyn

[Copy]

Mr Pepys's Enquiries to Mr Evelyn, relating to Navall Matters

[July 7, 1680]

Enquiries.

Instances of any Nationall Mistakes either new or old, whether at home or abroad in ye over Valueing their owne Knowledge or Force, or undervalueing those of other Countrys, and may not ye Ill Success of ye Spaniards in 88 bee in some measure Charged uppon a Mistake of this Kind in refference to us, as ours seems to be at this day in that against ye Moores in Barbary?

Instances of any Considerable Inventions or particular peeces of Knowledge, Whether in trade, science, or otherwise, Wherein we may rightly Value our Selves before our Neighbours?

Books of Stratagem & particularly Navall?

Why should other Nations more Ancient in their Navall actions then Wee, be thought less Inventive & Improv'd then us in the art of Navigation, While they are found soe much to outdo us, in all other arts, viz., Architecture, Painting, etc, and most other parts of humane Knowledge, whether for use or Pleasure

Instances of any Defeats anciently given us at Sea, or Invations made uppon our Land by Forrein^{rs} from the Roman Conquest upwards, to this day and more Especially from ye French

Who was Genebelli that built ye Block Houses in 88 at Gravesend, and first used y^e stratagem about three years before of Fire Boats at ye Siege of Antwerp

Who was Henry ye 8$^{th's}$ Engin^r in y^e Castles he built, & have wee ever had any Considerable Ingen^{rs} of our owne Country.

Queen Elizabeths forbidding King Henry ye 4th of France to build any new Ships, may not actions of his implying y^e Contrary be Instanced in,

Q:, y^e Records in y^e Great Wardrobe L Walsinghams words

The History of D. Dudley, And of Gabot, And the Fight at Lepanto, The Date and Author of The old Prologue.

Notable Ignorances of a Nation, Such as the burning of a B:^{pp} for asserting ye Antipodes.

32.

Evelyn to Pepys

[Copy]

Mr Evelyn to Mr Pepys, in answer to the preceding Queries

Wednesday Night after ye Musique
July ye 7th 1680

I will begin this Night, (Late as it is) to pay Mr Pepys: Some Tribute for ye Loss of his time, in Divirting me this afternoone, and when ever I waite upon him, and interrupt his more Serious affaires.

To the first Enquiry a Volume might be Compiled to Discover the Mistakes both in under and overvalueing our owne, and others Knowledge, Force, and Exploits, beyond y^t of other Nations, as far almost as wee can deduce the Sea adventures of former ages from Authentique Testimony, and much more Might wee have knowne, had wee the writings of Philo, Romanus, the Rhodian (as Suidas makes him) which are Perished, and Supplied to us out of ye Fragments in Cal: Rodoginus & Some fewe others, and as to undertakings uppon ye Opinion of our owne Dexterity & Virtue above our Neighbors I do not see y^t wee have much to boast of, at the foot of ye Reckoning, when wee shall have Discounted, For ye Mischiefe wee have received, from ye first Invation of ye Romanes, till our Shamefull Disgrace at Chatham,—I need not tell you what the Saxons, danes, & Normans did, But you shall find that none of them ever Landed on us with any Considerable Force, But they Caryed the whole Island (if they persisted) unless Some unforeseene Disaster befell them which was not in humaine power to prevent, Such as ye Storme that Dissipated ye Spanish Armada —more than the soe Celebrated Fireships of Sr Francis Drake, The Number otherwise of Men and Vessels being Certainly Sufficient for that Expedition & Design'd attempt, Soe as wee may Justly Sing, Non Nobis Domini, non Nobis, pray what have wee Gotten by our Late warr wth ye Hollanders, whome Albemarle did Soe Dispise, and yet tis Certaine wee have Infinite advantages of Ports & havens, to goe in and refitt, Lett us remember, how not onely Carthage, But Some little Common Wealths & Citty's in Greece, Contested Ages, the power of almost universall Monarchs, with [1] those who [2] overran all ye worth besides, and that wee have not ben Subject to those frequent Invasions of former times, is onely due to ye Care of those Princes who Succeeded the Conqueror, and yet the Streingth did then Consist more in hyred Ships, than Such as wee had built at home, till all Latter ages: Indeed Egbert, and his Successors began to furnish themselves with Numbers hardly to be Credited, Edgar tis Said had a Navy of neere 4000, But after all ye Danes began their Expedition but with 35 Ships, and after wth 84 with which they Infested our Coasts neere 200 yeares: Egelred ordered that every 300 hides of Land Should Sett forth Ship, which amounted Indeed to a numerous but unsuccessefull Fleete; Since ye Cuonquest the French in King Johns time Came into England with neere 700 Ships; But were indeed united by ye Barrons: In

[1] Manuscript reads *"and"* scratched out and *"with"* inserted.
[2] Manuscript reads "who *who*."

Edward ye 3^r wee were worsted by them, when they burnt Southampton, But their greatest Navy was in ye Reigne of our 2^e Richard, (which is Said even by our owne writers) to Consist of 1000 Saile mann'd by 600000 Soldiers tho it Came to Nothing, yet not Long after they did us infinite Mischeif all ye South Coasts over, and Such another Fleet for men, tho but of 200 Vessells, Invaded ye Isle of White in Henry ye 8th time, from which it may be Computed of how much water Burthen and Capacity they were Compared to those Superior in Numbers, Though I think it were not hard to Demonstrate, how former ages, did much Exceed ye Latter even in that particular, how Could they else beare from 2 to 15 banks of Oares on a syde? and when one of their Biremes computed to be neare of 600 Tunns, perhaps those might Rather be for Pomp than use, But how Soe many Oares could be Contrived, you will See in y^t Excellent Critic Palmerius, uppon ye Antient Greek Authors, Philopaters Vessell had 4000 men at oares, and what Numbers those of Xerxes Caryed will be found in Herodotus, Thycidedes, and I think in Pliny.

Now as to Inventions, (which is your second Querie), remitting you to Polydor Virgil. Pancirella; Britania, Baconica, Doctor Plat, when he Speaks of what any English man has produced, that ever was of Oxford Uniuersity (most worthy your perusall) you may please to Consult Sr Richard Bakers Collections, Especially for ye Learned men and benefactors, & for those trancendencies, you Desir'd to know wherein wee Exceeded other Nations, (if I mistake not) Peter Hylin has Spoken Something: you will in ye meane time recon our women, Horses, Dogs, Cocks, Rabits, Artichock, Tinn, Lead, Wool, Black Lead, red marking Stone, Oaker, Oakes, Herrings, Paintings in Miniature, Musitians on ye Viol de Gamba, & now of late Joyners, Carvers, Lock Smiths, Engine for Weaving Stockins &c Ribbon, Fullers, earth, Sea, & Scotch, Coale, Rings of Bells money, Bowling greens, Taverns, Inns, pinns, & Variety of Religions, I Name them all promiscuously for I have not time to Range them in order, and therefore proceed to Shipping, in which all Nations that have any ports Seeme to be piqu'd with the ambition of being the Inventors & of having Sovrainty on ye Seas, It were Loss of Time to report what I have published Concerning Minos of Crete, the Syrians, Egyptians, Cypnote, Rhodians, Phoenicians, Assyrians, who Succeeded the Egyptians, the Persians, Vanquisht by the Greeks & Macedonians, then the Romans, Jews, Moors, Arabs renoun'd once Asia & africa: I Come therefore to ye Latter among whome ye Italians & Portugese do not agree who were first in this Art, Whilst ye Spaniard pretends himselfe equall to them all, & the English, Normans, Danes, Superior; and this Leads me to ye 3^d Enquirie, and truly tis hardly imaginable how Nations Soe much Celebrated for their Navall Actions and Exploits should be Less Inventive in ye Art of Navigation who soe far outdid us both in ye Liberall and Politer Illiberal arts as to the actions and Exploits at Sea, Those of Corinth Doubtless were ye First of any we Read of, who fought upon ye waters if Thycededes may be Credited, as I think he may, wee have after them those vast Fleets of the asyrians, then of ye persians, which Darius & Successor Xerxes Equiped to ye number of 5600 Vessels Covereing the Hellispont, Though I fancy they Could not be of any great bulke, their Antagonists, (the Athenians), being open & without any Deck (see Diadorus Seculus) Such were Likewise those of ye Great Allexander, built on ye River Indus, To put to Sea in ye Great Ocean In all a 1000, But of which 800 Very Slight, Indeed, those of Athens, before Darius Alarm'd them, had not 60 Gallies, and they Ilmann'd, Nor had they any harbours Considerable, Til Themistocles, that brave Captaine made those three Comodious parts mentioned by Pausanius, built them Stouter Shipps, and Encouraged them to use ye Seas, t'wer worth your time to read in Diodorus, by what Adress he perswaded them & obtained that Glory from the Lacedemonians, There wee shall heare what Aristides accomplished What Pericles did with good pay to ye Seamen warring against ye Persians, How the Athenians became Soveraignes of ye Seas, braving it with 300 Galleys, and bravely Succoureing those of Cicily—Licurgus Equiped neare 500, and it was in those 3 harbours where they had the ἐπινειον ναυστάθμον σπλοθήκην or σκενοθήκην [3] Stations, yards, Docks Arsenals & Stores, which Certainely are marks of ye Greatness of a people and power at Sea, Such as for-

---

[3] Evelyn confused his accents in these Greek words which should read: ἐπίνειον ναυ'σταθμον ὁπλοθήκγν or ὁκευοθύκην.

ERRATA: MR. PEPYS AND MR. EVELYN

Page 124, line 33. Read ἐπίνειον ναυστάθμον ὁπλοθήκην or σκενοθήκην.
Page 124, footnote 3. Read ἐπίνειον ναύσταθμον ὁπλοθήκην or σκευοθήκην.
Page 125, line 9. Read τριηράρχος στρατήγος & πολέμαρχος.
Page 125, footnote 5. Read τριήραρχος στρατηγός πολέμαρχος.

merly were the Venetians, whose Arsenal is at this day the most Glorious thing of that kind in ye world, Though tis reported the French kings comes Very neare it, Over those had the Athenians their Majestrates, Storekeepers, Masters of attendants, etc here Herodotus, Thycidedes, Plutarch &c are to be Consulted and I think Budear, or the Pendects [4] gives you the Commissioners and other officers, who Delivered ye new built Vessell at ye place of Rendevouz, to ye Praeter or General, and there you'll see who were made τριηράρχος στρατήχος & πολέγχεχος [5] Captaines and Millitary officers with ye number of their Souldiers as ye Occation required for Such were Nicias, Demosthenes, Alcibiades, Pericles Cimon etc, and Some times one alone, for Soe was Euribiades, General at ye Saluminian and Decresa Bataille against Xerxes Fleete of 500000 men, it was doutless a brave and Noble Designe That Allexander undertooke, When after his Last Victory over Darius, he would have Discov'red the Asiatic and Indian Sea, and Soe have Circled the whole Globe of the earth Under the Direction of Nearchus, Onesicritus, Diogneses, [   ] [6] etc and had it in his Vast thoughts to have sett forth a Fleete of a 1000 Ships upon ye Report of ye Carthaginean power at Sea, But Death put a period to this though not to ye atempts of Some of his Successors, Nicanor, Seleneus etc when Patroclus went to Discover further into the Indies, But above all Renoun'd were the Ptolomy's, Particularly Philadelphus, by ye Discoverys which hath, Megastines the Dionissus made into those parts, and there is yet mention of ye Commission which was given to Dicearchus to measure ye Medeteranian, But S^r I groe Tedious to you, and will therefore now Contract my Sailes, and Come Nearer home, How this Island was first peopled, I had rather you should read out of y^t Excellent Little book written by our Countriman Twyne, where having the figments of King Lud and his Trojans, you will See his Conjecture about ye rupture of an Isthmus That in all Probabillity might formerly have united this Land to ye Continent, and as to what Confirmes our being Visited by the

---

[4] Reading doubtful.
[5] Evelyn again confused his accents. The Greek should read: τριήραρχος στρατηχός πολέμαρχος.
[6] Word blotted.

Ships of other Nations, How the Pheonicians & Tirians were the most famous planters of Colloneys wherever they Came, how they Crept to Gades thence to our Countrey, for Gold, Silver, Tinn & Plunder, & though that booke were written in Henry ye 8th time, Dialogue Wise, it is yet in Soe pure and Chast a Stile, and with that Judgment, that you will be Exceedingly Delighted with it, and track Mr Cambden who has not been a Litle obliged to the Author, I also mention it the Rather that you may See what Learned persons Some of our Countrymen were, at that time, you will alsoe take Notice how handsome a Character he gives our Henry ye 7th, but to proceed The Pheonecians, Came first as far as Utica, Hippo, Lophes, & in Africa, To Thebes in Greece, then into Spaine, not forgetting Carthage, which I should first have Named, as their Deriveing their Dominion, and from whence they made most ample Descovreys even as far as the Equenoxeal, and Some you know tell us that Hanno Came about even to Arabia; there was a journall of these renowned Captaines written in ye Punic toungue, and afterwards translated into Latin by Injunction of ye Roman Senat, which is now lost ah what pitty, They alsoe Dispatched Himilo with a like Comission & Fleete to Discover ye rest of Europe, and they were those Carthaginians or Phenicians, (for tis all one) who planted the Coasts of Spaine built another Carthage there for Security of there Fleetes, and had for ought apeares, held that whole Country to this day, but for the Romans, who were themselves beated out by ye Vandals Goths and Sarracens, But not onely grediness of Riches Caused those and other people to wander thus and undertake adventure of Danger, But ye more frequent and Terrible Deluges, Earthquakes, Conflagrations, Plagues, and warre, with which god Almighty Chastised ye vicious heathen world in those Early dayes for Else hardly would they have been perswaded, to Change those warmer Climats, for the more Northern & uncultivated places of france and Britain, But of this enough, and perhaps to much, I returne therefore to Inventions againe, and to Shew what Incredible things they did by their Dilligence and Expedition, wee read of the whole Fleete in which Duillius was General in the First punic warr, that it was built and Sett out in five and fifty days, and against Hioro 200 saile in

APPENDIX

45 dayes, and within ye Space of two monthes Scipio's Fleete in ye 2^d punic war was built, the wood and Timbers growing wthin that Space, But of this I have Spoken more at Large in my Silva, therefor their Curious Forme and Navall Architecture, There were two, the Salaminia & Paralus, which were Called the Sacred, the first Consisted of 30 oares these are reported to Conduct Theseus to Creete, and this was that Reverend Vessell, which wee read was Soe often rebuilt as it Decay'd (you know ye Story) and preserv'd to ye time, of Demetrious Phalerius, how Gloriously She was Carved and Adorned, how she Sail'd to Delos to a Sollemne Sacrifice, and that from ye Day of her Setting out to her returne, twas not Lawfull to put any Mallifactor to Death in Athens, Diodorus and other authors informe us Paralus, the other Ship had Likewise her priviledges apart which Concerned the mariners & officers too long to rehearse, and I should not have mentioned those things but to comply with your Enquires because they will be Instances of ornement to Such a worke as I hope you have your thoughts on: and to which among other good Authors Pausanias will Contribute more, And though this Last Vessell had Nine benches of Oares on each syde and 9 upon each bench, I do not think it is Comparable to ye Venetian Bucentora, in which ye Duke and Senate Espouse the Adriatic on assention day, at which Ceremony I have been present, What Vessels wee have built of this Nature you better know then I ten thousand times, and what our Neighbours have Sett out for pomp, as ye Sweden Megalesia, the Spaines Llanio Sprito, the French Kings that when built could not be Launched, the Great Henry in Henry ye 8th Time was of a 1000 tunns, I had quite forgot ye Ship of Hiero which had gardens and orchard etc in it. Soe gloriously Discried by Atheneus, and I Say nothing of those reported to be in China fearing them fables, Now I should Come to Authors, Engineers, Stratagematistes, and other Shorter queres in your paper, amongst which I find that Comon Tradition of Henry ye 4th of France, being prohibited to build any Ships of warr by queene Elizabeth, it doth not occur at present, where I have read it onely this I know in Contradiction of it, that he did not Neglect his Interest at Sea as apeares by his many projects for trade, and performances at Marseilles, all that Richelieu & his

Successor pursued being projected by this great prince, as you may See in Morisotus Preface and haveing Said this I will honestly Declare to you, what, after all my Enquires, (betweene you and I) Seemes to be ye Case as to our pretence to the Dominion of ye Sea and Fisherys, and this I will the rather adventure to Enlarge a Litle on, because it is a point you Cañot Leave untouched, and perhaps may gather Something usefull to you, though the Doctrine be Soe heterodox to what I myselfe have published, and why I am not ashamed to make this retraction, I Shall Signifie in ye Close, I acknowledge in my booke, I Sought industriously to assert our tytle, and as pro hic et nunc it became mee, the Circumstances of that time, and his Majestyes Express Command to mee Considered. But between friends when Such like topics are used, (as Sometimes even in Parliaments they were) tis plaine they were passed over upon Important reasons, (But tis now neere three in the morning) I will Sleep a Litle, and finish what I have more to Say, before I waite on you to ye Philosophers this day, for wide day it is Thursday ye 8th July. To begin where I left now I am up againe—

Supposing the old Brittaines did prohibit forreinirs to Come into their Countrey, it infers not any Claime of Dominion in ye Narrow, but a Jealosy rather over their proper Coasts, nor read wee that they ever practiz'd it over ye Gaules, (the Chinesses as I Sujested to you yesterday, forbad all to Come into their Countrey, for Political reasons, are they therefore Lords of the oriental Seas, or ever did wee heare they pretended soe to be? As to king Arthur (abating what is fabulous) that is his Legendary Dominion ye comes littoris Saxoniis and the like, either it inferrs to much or nothing at all, his Dominion Streched to Denmark, Sweeden, Norway, & Iseland, have wee therefore any right of Claime to those realmes at present? why then to ye Seas? againe admit ye most, Cannot Dominion be Lost or Extinguished? was not his rather a Momentary Conquest or Excursion rather then any Establish'd Dominion? was it not Lost to ye Danes? had they not all ye Characters of Dominion Imaginable? (read our Histories) Lords of our Seas, four Shores, and the tribute of Danegelt—from England & Ireland, Soe as if ever there weere a reall Dominion of ye Seas in ye world, wee might yield these people to have had it, and if their tytle Can-

APPENDIX 129

not be Extinguished by Subsequent Revolutions, I much question whether ours will ever be Evinced, The Story of King Edgar is Certainly horribly fabulous, and the pretended deds I feare as Spurious, truly if fforeinge Cronicles had been as much Stoff'd with his renowne, as with King Arthers, more Credit were to be given to it, in ye meane time what is said of Althelred is against us, Since tis Evident he paid the Danegelt as a tribute to them, and Setled it to that end, Tis a Q^{ry} whether the Scots Seas, & Scotland too be not a fee to England, Since with as good reason wee Might Chalenge it, if the produceing of roles, records, and acts of Parliam̃ts, and of Statuts to that purpose were of any Importance, because wee Can Shew many more to that Since then in the other Case; But how would then Scots take it, and what become of their Laws about Fishing, Tis declared in our Laws that wee are Lors of ye Four Seas and tis Soe adjudged in our Courts, as to those borne uppon those Seas, and yet the Parliament of Scotland can Lay a Tax on our Fishermen, (as I am assured) wch is a Considerable argument against us, I neaver read that our Kings ever prohibited any to fish on ye Coasts of Scotland, or Charged them with usurpation, for takeing toll or Custome for ye Herring Fishing, though the papers wch were given mee to Contract, and insert in my booke, faine would have it Soe, The truth is the Licences, (which I mention as from Scarbrough) were onely to fish on ye Dogger banck Such English as were to fish on ye Scotch-Seas about Orkney, Shetland, Iseland, and Fero etc did all take Lycence from ye Kings of Norway at Bergen or Northbarum and this Jurisdiction, and Soverenty undouted of ye Norwergien Kings, is recognized by our Parliament in a Statute of 8th: Henry 6th, and by innumarable treaties between ye two Crownes, even within a Century of yeares, and if Soe, Consider how fraile a proofe is ye famous roll pro hominibus Hollandiae, and how it is to be Limited in it selfe (by the history and occation that Caus'd it) to ye Narrow or Chañell onely Tis alsoe to be Considered, that ye Danes pretended at Breda, that ye Cession of ye Scots fishery about Orkney Shetland, was neaver made to King James, on ye Mariage to Queene Ann (as ye vulgar Story goes nor any time before to any Scoch king, and Supposing there were any Such Authentick deedes it were better to fix the Fishery (we contend for) even in ye Dutch then either to Suffer it to be regulated by the Decrees of a Scotch Parliament, or transfer it to that Nation, whome I take to be an hardier, and more industrious people, and you may remember, what old George Cock was wont to say that it was incompatible with our English ease, and Luxury, to Sett up that Trade to ye prejudice of our Neighb^rs who were better husbands and fared harder: As to the vast trade and multitude of English Ships by the History of ye Hanse Townes, their priviledges and Strength in England, one shall find (as before I noted) that for ye bulk, most of our Navies were hired Ships of ye Venetians, Genoveses. & Ausiatics 'til Q Eliz—whose number I think exceed not much above 24 good Vesells Then ye right of Passes and Peticōns was founded on another parte of ye Jus Gentium rather then our pretended dominion of the Seas, which (to Speake ingeniously) is hard to find expressly acknowledged in any Treaty with fforraigners And as to the Fishing of ye Dutch without Licence, the Intercursus magnus Soe boasted was a perpetuall Treaty, and was made with ye People as well as the Princes of Burgundy and Soe as to be obligatory, tho' they rejected their princes as we Se most of them did, and as they might according to the Letus Introitus wch I mention. and that the Dutch are Stil (and by Q. Eliz were Soe declared to be) a Pars Contrahens after their Revolt and defection (yee abjuracōn of Spaine) does much invalidate ye proceedinge of King James & Char's: who both Signed y^e *Intercursus,* and were in truth included thereby tho' they had not done it. The nature of prescription too would be Looked into, as well when it makes against us, as for us, and therefore it Should be enquired whether Q Eliz did not first affect the Mare Liberum in opposition to the Danes, and whether his present Matie has not done it at Jamaica against ye Spaniarde, pray consider ye Seale of that Admiralty. To say truth when I writt my booke (which was but for preface to ye Peice I told you of, and a Philologicall exercise to Bspeake ye Reader, and gratify the present persons and Circumstances) I could not clearly Satisfy myselfe in Sundry of those particulars, nor find really that ever ye Dutch paid Toll, or tooke License to fish in Scottland after ye Contest. Indeed (as I relate) they tooke Browne who came to exact it and detaind him in Holland severall Months, but I find not they ever paid penny for it tho ye Papers Sr Joseph Williamson put into my hands Speake of Assize herring; Nor find I that any Rent (whereof I calculate ye Arrears) for permission to Fish was ever fixt by both partyes; and Soe cannot be properly calld a Settled Rent, this would therefore be exquisitly Searched into, and perhaps both for these and diverse other particulars a thro' search in ye Paper Office may give better Light if there have been any due care taken to collect and digest Such important mattere, wch I much fear Seeing it lyes in such disorder, when I had permission to make use of what I thought fitt upon that occasion. As to ye yeare 1637 & 38 you cannot but see through the Intrigue, the equipping that formidable Fleete, that they were more to awe France than Terrify Holland, and that any Licences were taken in those yeares, I cannot be convinc'd of, that of 36 being but a Single Act of force on particular men, the States never owning them in it, and you know the Admirale Darp was Chasheered for not quarreleing it wth Northumberland, & our Conducte and Licensies flatly refused in 37 when Capt Feild came. finaly (for I grow very tedious to one soe far more inlightned then I am) when K James did fix his Chambers, did he not either renounce the English Soverainty of the Seas, or Violate therein his League wth Spaine (as that Nation urg'd it, pleading that ye Brittish Seas were *teritorium Domini Regis,* but he did not the latter, nor am I Single in this Deduction: In a word the whole Argument of the Fishery is too controvertable, to be too peremptorily decided by the Penn, and on many other accounts, and as I said a project uselesse: and therefore might wth much more ease and facility be Supply'd by encourageing our Fishing at Newfound Land; Lastly as to our Comerce in Generall by all that I could observe, dureing the Short time of my being at ye Councill, where I a litle looked into those matteres (now utterly laid asside) concluded it a very Vaine thing, to make any probable, certaine, or necessary proposall aboute Trade, not but y^t it might be infinitly improv'd if Princes and people, did Steadily unanimously, and wth a Publique Spiritt (& as our advantages, of Scituation etc prompts) Sett themselves honestly, and with industry aboute it, but for that as things goe, and are hitherto manag'd (since Q E. time) the whole Advantage this Nation receives therebye, is evidently carryed on more by Antient Methods, and ye Sedulites of private persones than by any real publique encouragem^t, and as to ye pres^t (whatever we boast) it certainly Languishes under insupportable dificulties, and does not stand upon a Solid Base Soe long as we are in this uncertaine Condicōn, among o^r Selves at home: (Thus S^r, I chuse to convey you, my 2^d & more Serious Reflecc̄ons, upon a Subject, wch in your excellent work Cannot escape yor discussion, Speaking of the importance of Shipping, and I doe it wth all manner of Selfe denyall imaginable after what I have publish'd to ye Contrary, by wch you may conclude how Suspicious wise men ought to be of other Histories how Specious Soever—unlesse where there is demonstracōn, y^t the Authours had noe interest of their owne to Serve, and were not influenc'd, by their Superior or publick cry; Nor whilst I make this Confession to you does it raise any blush, wch certainly it would have done, had I publish'd any thing on this Subject, but what I rec^d out of Authours before me, or from ye paperes which were Sent me to peruse and reduce into ye Method you see, wch was in truth to usher in ye pretence we would have had to iustify, an unsuccesfull (I would I could say a Righteous) quarrell, but that I was not to be Judge of. And now tho I should not be prudent to destroy and pull downe what I have built, if it may Serve ye present turne Yett were I to begin that work againe (as now inform'd) I would temper ye Cement after another manner, and write lesse magisterially that is more ingeniously. But you will Still consider the time and Circumstance in all Events. I have therefore my Excuse (as to you) that one of ye most pious and usefull bookes, of that Learned and excellent Father St *Augustine* was his *Retractations:* you have mine in this part of my Letter, and for that ye best part of it went to ye profession of my being yor very humble Servt: and to this I would Subscribe my name, and make an end but that Something remaines to be said upon yor other enquiries First,—Who Ganebelli was I have told you, now as to H. 8th Fortificacōnes, 'tis evident he made Severall Bulwarks on ye Sea Coast anno 1539 (if I mistake not ye yeare)—upon Apprehensione of Invasiones, when he fell out with the Pope, but who were his Engineers I doe

APPENDIX 133

not know unlesse S^t a Cicilia whome Palsoe mencōnd to you:—
As to ye exploit done on ye bridge at Antwerpe Famianus Strada, will give you a more particular, and the Mercurius Gallo belgius of that yeare wch I think I have by me tho' I am not certaine: Except Dr Dee I learn not who Q Eliz: made use of, but there was a Neapolitan Sent from Spaine privately by Sr Nicholas Throgmorton, who tis probable might Serve her; in ye meane time, tho' K John built diverse Castles on ye Coaste and Midland Places dureing the Barons Warre, I read of very few or none built after H 7th came to the Crowne and had Suppress'd the Barōns, but in former times there was very good reason to defend our Selves, the French continually molesting our Coaste, from ye Raigne of Willm ye Conquerour, even as farr as Gravesend, which they tooke & burnt, and therefore, I suppose that Fort to be antienter then H. 8 they alsoe invaded the Isle of Wight, burnt Ryenay, Portsm^e, Dartmouth, and Plymouth. But whilst I Speake of Engineers, I cannot forbear to provoake your curiosity (if you have not consider'd it already) to read ye discription our Hollingshead has made of the building or Repairs of Dover Peere, it being the first Mole work, I read of in this Nation, because you will finde it Soe particular, as if you were now Spectator of ye Worke and in truth I was much affected with it, it is describ'd Soe warmly, and gives us an Idea of the worthy industry of that Age viz: Q Eliz: you'l finde it in his fol 2^d Vol and in it diverse observable things. The first Engineer Seemes to have been one Thompson a Preist (call'd Sr John Thompson, as then ye maner was, and yett is in our Universityes to Styl Batchelors of Art) who first undertooke it in H: 8 time, there you shall read of one Jos: Young who invented ye way of transporting huge Stones: etc, and how like Americus Vespatianus) he began wth an Egshell, there youl finde another Engineer, calld Jo Trew, who intended a Mole of Stone, like that of Tangier instead of Wood. Ferdinand Pains Succeeded him, (a Jersy Man I fancy) and there alsoe of a Cofin-dam and mencōn made of a Peter Pett, and one Baker Shipwrighte who were for the Timber Wall.

Sebastian Gabot or Cabot was borne at Bristoll his Parents of Genoa, and was Sent out by H 7th and left a Chart of his Passage to Cathaia, wch hung up in the Privy Gallery at Whitehall long time after, what become of it I cannot tell, Enquire if Chistings has it.

The Fight at Lepanto I charge my Selfe to shew you with other things of that nature when you have an idle afternoone to Spend in ye Country, the booke of that Colleccon being too unweildy to remove.

Walsingams words are to be found in Hackluit—as I remember, when I Speake of ye Prologue, or from ye fountaine in his History.

I mencond Sr Walter Rawleigh's confidence wth the charge of 200000£ for but two yeares to Subdue the greatest power in ye World (wch then was Spaine and the Turk) and you will finde it with diverse other worthy Remarks in Sr W. R's history if you Search the Tables.

As to Trade it were a noble Colleccon, could we procure all that has been printed (which would make a very usefull and considerable Volume, because for most part publish'd by wise and knowing men) Since H. 8th time to this they are comonly in ye bulk but of Pamphletts, but in my opinion of much esteem: out of them it would be enquired, when ye English Staple was remov'd into Brabant being 100 yeares and more Since fixed at the Dort, and this Leads me to your last Queerie what bookes are to be consulted, for those particulars First Boxhornius has written an history of the Ansiatic Townes where you'l find in what Condicon and Creditt Holland was for Trafique and Soe in ye Danish Annales.

Concerning Shiping and Sea matters, twere good to read Pausanius in Attice. Jssodori Originali de Navigatione Litius Gyraldus de re Navali; Posinus e Antiquities, Ferrier (whome yesterday you enquired for) de re Navali also, tho' some of those I fancy Scarce ever Saw the Sea, but for asmuch as there are many worthy antiquityes, and other passages fitt to illustrate, and adorne a Consumate peece, these are not to be neglected; I cannot here but note, that the French pretend to have had Admiralls from ye very foundacon of their Monarchy, even at the time of the Antient Gaules, but in earnest whoever can name us any before Euguerant de Caucy aboute ye time of Phillip Sonn of Louis, must Violate all good history This by the way only, Bessomius has his Theatrum Machinarum, (w^ch

APPENDIX

I have in Spanish) wth Beroaldus's notes and addition, Since publish'd wth Paschalis's Suppliment in wch Some Enquire for the Construction of Moles; weighing up Sunck Ships and other invenc͠ons of that Sort.

Rumelli you had yesterday, in your hands at Mr Scotts in wch are few that Signify to Ships. What those of Causee are I will Show you, it is a noble booke but not for your turne I think unless it be Curiosity, I need not mind you of Vogetius and Frontinus where you will find what was invented for old Fireworkes, but not Soe accurately and usefully as in Monsr Mallette 3^d Volume i.e. Le Travaux de Mars publish'd aboute 8 yeares Since, and highly worth your haveing, tho I doe not much preferr it to our Country Man Cyprian Lucars his appendix to Nich. Tartaglia an Italian, whome I should have conjectur'd to have been one of H. 8th: Engineers (of wch you Soe enquire) and to whome he dedicates his booke but for Some passages in his Epistle, was not o^r late Sr Jonas Moore left Something of this Subject, I meane concerning Fireworks and Artillery, for my part I doe not finde much has been added Since Lucar tho near an hundred yeares Since unlesse in ye Magnitude of Bombs Of this Subject alsoe has written Grolamo Catanea aboute ye Same time, and it were good to compare them, and what has been improv'd.

For Lifting Engines have you ye Invenc͠on of Dominico Fontana who in ye Raigne of Sixtus Quintus Pope, erected ye Gulias [7] or Obilisks that had been prostrate near 1000 yeares for want of an Engineer.

The French Edition of Recreations Mathematicall with the English *Bates* may be perused alsoe Baptiste Portia but above all Galilio of the most Subtiler parts of the Mechanics, and there is extant of old Archimedes's Treatise de ijs quae vehuntur in aquis published by Comandinus wth a Coment

Explicatio des Termes de Marine was printed at Paris above 40 yeares Since.

Dr Gilber, our Ridly, and Weird of ye Loadstone not forgetting Kircher.

And I am sure you have Sr W. Ralisses select Essayes upon the

---

[7] Probably the architectural term *gula* or *gola* (see N. E. D.).

first Ivencon of Shiping a litle 8º booke and now the other day has not our Minister Mr Golden presented you wth his Trinity Monday Sermon a Learned peice: One Baillott, Sett forth a Small Vol: in French aboute artificiall fireworks, and Soe did Monsr: Prousel: I name them all promiscuously, as they come to my memory, for I protest I write all these two Sheetes without booke (and should I think) doe Soe till night if by it I may doe you any Service, and now I am going to Speake wth Sr Den: Gauden who has made me Stay within all this morning: Pardon this confus'd Scribble, this desultory and imethodicall Trifle and Love

S^r: Your most humble Servt:
                        J Evelyn.

I have noe time to read what
I have written, and am Sure 'tis Swarming
wth Faults, for I am very Gidy headed,
but if it doe not Serve to Stay your
Stomach till I come, and y^t within one
quarter more Stay not for me longer.

33.

Evelyn to Pepys

[Copy]

A Letter from Mr Evelyn to Mr Pepys concerning ye Battle of Lepanto & ye Antiquity of Shipping

Whitehall 6th 7^br 1680

S^r

Since this Paradisian Weather has not all this while incited you downe the River, and that being not Soe very well in health as I could waite on my friends in London untill now, you will easily excuse my not giving you a more accurate Acco^t of the Battell of Lepanto, which you will finde in Severall Histories of that time

APPENDIX

especially in ye Life of Pius Quintus, written by Girolumo Catena, where, at the end you'l finde, an exact List of all that Armada on both Sides, with the Comanders and Orders of Squadrons. The Booke is printed at Mantua, 1587. Something of it is Said also in the History of the Knights of Malta, as farr as concerned that particular Order, in a large Volume, but not Soe fully as in ye other. And now I will give you what has occurr'd to me, in Some Scattering Notes, by me written downe in my Adversaria, at Several times without any Method.

The first mony I finde Said to be Stampt was that of Janus's head, and, on ye Reverse a Ship. The History you have in Macrobius Satur: 1: i: for when Sailing wth Saturne he in recompence taught that Hero Husbandry and how to meliorate Fruites, he was rec^d as partner in ye Empire which occasion'd this Medaile to be Stamp'd. It was with this farthing, that the little Boyes were wont to play at Capita and Navia, which we now, call Cross and Pile (Pile is an obsolate French word for a Ship, and thence Pilott) See the Antiquity of that Childish Play, the oldest I read of but ye Coine it Selfe was called Retitus Numus.

Amongst Cups and Gobletts to drink in Some were of old made like Boates, and ye Beakes of Ships, The Greekes had their Carchesia or Cymbia (a diminutive of Cymba) as the Romans. Cape Macony Carchesia Bacchi and Hic duo rite mero, libans Carchesia—Baccho and of Boates In ferimus tepido Spumantia Cymbia Lacte, The Carchesia Soe call'd a. navali re. See it described by Asclepiades, quoted by the same Authour Li 5 and it Seemes there were diverse other Cupps, amongst the merry Greekes of this Sort but ye Cyssymbium was a wooden Vessell, comonly of Ivy and Such a Cupp was sometimes used by the Greeke Poets—figuratively for a Ship See Menander in Nanclero, they feign'd that Hercules was transported in one of those as far as Gades: Pherecydes is made ye Reporter, but rather in truth in a Ship cui Syphonomen for all these were Navigiorum Vocabula.

You have Hiero's great Vessell (for enough of Small Craft) describ'd in Athenaeus & Casaubons notes to the full, he had Gardens and Fruite trees Floating, Tenis Courts and what not: But if it be true, what I finde of the Spanish Carracas, or (as they call them) Naes des Indias, they were not much Inferior for Largness, Some of them being built wth six Decks or Stories, and all of halfe pike height to ye Roofe. Some of these Vessells were 180 paces in Length, and forty in breadth, and have been knowne to carry from Spaine to ye Indies 500 Families, their Children, Servants, and Household Stuffs, with provision for a 6 months Voyage. The Passengers Living as in a Citty, yett unknown to one another, as if many miles distant.

I forgott to adde (as to ye Small but very curious Craft) that amongst the Reliques of the Cathedrall at Tolledo, there is shew'd a Ship wrought all out of Rock Chrystall, wth the very Cordage of the Same, Such of Ivory I have seen in other places wch is not Soe Curious.

(The Navigacone and exploits of the Portugueses are at Large in Hieron Osonius, both in Latine and French from Emanuel ye first 1496, to Sebastian ye first, wherein are all their Navigations, and Conquests of ye East Indies at Large worth ye perusall, I think you asked me about this)

Pray Consult ye Comentators on 27 Ezek: from ye 4th to ye 9th where you'll finde mencon'd Plancks of Firr, Masts of Cedar, Oake for Timber Speaking of the Tyrians, There's alsoe mencon of Pilotts, Caulkers, Mariners and Vessells, some soe rich, as to have ye Benches and Hatches (See in Margines) inlaid wth Ivory, and in y^t Chapter a wonderfull Acco^t of their early Trafique, the Critica at large will Satisfy you in this. But I tire you and therefore for this time (and till you open my mouth againe) conclude wth what I lately found reading over Dr Burnetts excellent history of our Reformation, that one of H. ye Eights excuses for ye demolition of ye Monasteries etc was ye building and fortifying of Ports in ye Chañell and other Places: See his 3^d: booke pp 269: 284 etc

            haec Raptim from
          S^r
                  Yo^r most humble Servt:
                  J Evelyn.

34.

Evelyn to Pepys

[Holograph]

S-C:^t 8-Jan-8 5/6

S^r,

I am sure that what you negotiate to bring about, cannot but obtaine in desired Effect; therefore as to M^r: Dūmers Concerne, I leave that to you with intire acquiescence: Indeed I think him worthy of y^r favour, for never in my Life have I observ'd a Young man (qualified as he is in his way, & susceptible of what can be wanting) lesse pragmatical, & of greater modesty; beside his so submissive, & cheerfull dedication of himselfe to his patron alone, which is a mark of his discretion, as well as of his duty.

Now S^r to the other part of y^r Lett^r: I cannot but think it a very venial fault (in the Cavalier you speake of) to Consigne a Wife to her owne Husband, whose Charmes (as I am told) are not at all extraordinary, before they be quite vanish'd & effeete: Mithinks he ought to give *You* thanks for making it so easie to him, & so decent: But (whatever the good man may faile in this particular) I am sure I am to pay you my most humble thanks for the honour you have don me, in making me ye proxy on so weighty a Negotiation, as in the Comands you mention; Be assur'd I shall take care to performe your trust with all fidelitie; but whether the Lady you speake of accept of y^r Substitute, because I represent Mr Pepys, I much doubt whether the whole Sex would be as kind (or rather I am sure the [1] would not) to Sixty, as to Fourty; were there no other Consideration (as there is a greate deale to the advantage of Mr Pepys) betweene the principle & the proxie:—But

S^r to leave this part of Gallantrie 'til we meete, & have opportunitie of proposing it to the Ladys: Receive from both your Proxies our reiterated Acknowledgemente (with the Augure of many happy

[1] They?

new-Years) for all your greate Civilities, but in particular for this last to

S^r

Y^r most obliged humble Ser^t

J Evelyn:

35.

Evelyn to Pepys

[Holograph]

[no date] [1]

S^r,

You were pleas'd not long-since, to say you would Continue to us the favour of Ordering that the Watch-man (whose station is at the Dore of his Ma^{tys} Yard, very neere my Stayers) should—as formerly he did, take Care of Clensing them, and the Causey, which, Since this Late, thô Short, Interruption, are allmost quite cover'd with mud, and made use-lesse by it: I come with the more assurance that I shall obtaine this kindnesse of you (without prejudice to his Mat^{ies} Service) Inasmuch as by our Articles, those stayers, & Casey are to be maintaind & repair by his Ma^{ty} during the terme of the Lease; and that in case they be neglected, they will soone require it: One thing more I make bold to mention, that in regard of the Passage (wholy reserv'd by me out of S^r D: Gaudens Lease) thrô which I consent that Workemen etc may at all times have recourse to y^e Mast-docks; it was mutualy agreed, that y^e Watchman who kept that doore, should also have a key to the stayers for the use of y^e $C\bar{o}miss^{rs}$ onely; so that there was to be no other intercourse thrô it, but to them and my family, for the more security of y^e Dock: In order to this, Such a Lock was promis'd should be put on, and will be so, and all the rest perform'd, when y^u shall please to signifie so much to y^r $c\bar{o}miss^r$ here, who, I am Sure, will be a kind Neighbour to us: As for the Watch-man, (who has Little to do a greate part of the day, but to walk about), it will be but a short exercise to him,

---

[1] Listed in the sales catalogue of S. J. Davey (1889) as June 1686.

when a foule tyde requires it, and I do not use at the yeares end to forget ye poore man. S^r, You will also think at some convenient time, to call for the Book, and give order that the Lease be impress'd & seald, which as yet it is not, thrô the unaccountable neglect of our late famous Admiralty, or Officers: This, I mention to prevent accidents, and I will tell you what I meane when I have the honor to see you, & how I merit for this Advertisement: But, I would derive all my greate Obligations from y^r kindnesse alone, who am
S^r, Y^r most faithful
humble Ser^t J. Evelyn

S^r, I should be glad to know when I might wait on you to my Ld Dartmouth, confident of giving all Satisfaction to his L^d on that other affaire: Be so kind to me as to let me know when you will also accumulate this favour on me.

36.

Pepys to Evelyn

[Holograph]

Tuesday morning.
April 1687.

S^r

Though my Lady bee out of towne (for which I am sorry) & that my Lady Tuke (to whom I owe ye favour) is not in present condition by ye death of her Father to take any share her selfe of it, yet I did not know but you might thinke it worth your while to make a stepp hither ab^t 8 this evening to heare Cefache; where you will bee most wellcome to
Y^r most humble Servant
S Pepys.

37.

Pepys to Evelyn

[Holograph]

Febr. 15th 1694/5

Dearest S^r

The Sent, as well as Noise, of Christmas is now over with you (I presume) soe as a Man may Greate you in the bas stile againe.

Wee have had 2 greate Vacancys fallen since wee last talked together; that in ye Church I am sure you & I shall thinke well fill'd; while the other in ye State fills it selfe. Fiat voluntas tua! And with this Interjection, lett mee give way to an occasion that won't lett mee goe on, & I would not loose this Conveyance for ye small prints that accompany this, leaveing ye rest to a further but speedy Day. I bid you Adieu & am as allways

Yours indefinitely
S Pepys.

38.

Hewer to Evelyn

[Holograph]

Clapham 13th September 1705

Sr

I have been honoured with yours of the 10th instant, and am sorry to finde the trouble I have occasioned you by my not being set cleare as I ought and intended to have been in my answer to your former. Mrs Skinners Annuity (concerning which you are againe pleased to enquire) is parcell of, and [ ]¹ and payable out of the proceed of the 12000 £ Fortune of Mr Jackson. Which Estate soe circumstanced being what you seeme to have little expectation of meeting with acceptance from the Young Lady's Relations; there remaines not Subject for Further Argument relating to the settlement proposed; Nor shall I therefore offer to trouble you with any. I have been prevented waiting upon you as I fully purposed by an Indisposition of some days; but will not faile to lay hold of the first opportunity of doing it, to make my excuse for having interested my selfe in an affaire yielding you noe greater satisfaction. I heartily congratulate you upon the neare approach of the Young Gentn your Grandson's Settlement, with so happy a prospect of Comfort to you, &, could have been very glad that matters had concurred to give me the like occasion upon the present Proposall. The enclosed beggs your admittance upon the same Subject, from Mr Jackson, who desires to joyne with mee in most humble Services and Respects, to your Lady & selfe, as well as intreating your Pardon to him, and

Sr

    Your very humble and most affectionate Servant
    Wm Hewer

¹ Word undeciphered.

39.

Jackson to Evelyn

[Holograph]

Clapham Septr 13th 1705

Hon^d S^r

Yours of ye 10th to Mr Hewer, discovering the Result of your Thoughts concerning ye Proposal lately made on my behalfe, has been communicated to me by him; Wherein, as becomes me, I acquiesce, without adding to my Presumption by my Importunitys. This Event, however unwelcome, is no more than what I had always endeavour'd to prepare myselfe for; having engaged in ye attempt with great diffidence of Success, & a just Consciousness of the disproportion between ye Merits of Mrs Evelin & one who had little in present to value himselfe upon, more than an honest Education & an inoffensive Life. I had indeed great Ambition to an Alliance of so consummate worth & Vertue as ye Family of Mr Evelin, & should have thought myself in ye highest degree happy in it; could Circumstances have been brought to suit: But your Last leaving me without hopes, of this, It remains only for me humbly to begg my Lady's & Your pardon for ye liberty I have used on this Occasion; to acknowledge ye many honours you have done me in ye Course of it; and to request, that as no one besides Yourselves & Mr Hatton has either by Mr Hewer or me been made privy to any part thereof, So You will please to let it rest with You, & grant ye Continuance of Your Friendship & Patronage, with ye same goodness as before to,

Hon^d S^r
Your most Obed. & most
humble Servt
Jackson

40.

Evelyn to Jackson

[Draft] [1]

Answer: 15. Sepr 1705

S^r

Upon Receite of Mr Hewers, and your most Civil Replys to mine, I have honestly & with all Ingenuity, declard to him, the onely Obstacle to this Important Affairs Conclusion, whilst that Incumbrance is thought to make the rest much too streite to Imbarke a family in (such is the present age) tho with the addition of the Portion, which is most of it in Land, in as good Condition as is any in England: S^r I am extreamly sorry for an Interuption, which I assure y^u [we now make w] [2] no small regrett, whilst I must ever remember the [ ] [3] & greate Obligation I have to y^r Late Worthy Unkle: Be assurd S^r (whether y^u had given me that Caution or not,) I should exactly have observd it who am, & shall [4] ever Continue

    S^r
      Y^r most faithfull
    & most humble Servant.
      J E.

41.

Evelyn to Hewer

[Draft] [5]

Answer: 16 S^{br}—1705

S^r

I should be most sensibly touch'd, did any thing of this Proposal receive the least interruption from me or my Wife, who shall ever

---

[1] Written in Evelyn's hand on the reverse side of Jackson's letter to Evelyn, September 13, 1705.

[2] Reading doubtful.

[3] Word undeciphered.

[4] Evelyn wrote "must" above "shall" without erasing "shall."

[5] Written in Evelyn's hand on the reverse side of Hewer's letter to Evelyn, September 13, 1705.

esteeme Mr Jacksons Person & extraordinary Acc̄omplishments of far more Value than his Estate, were it a great deale more and am therefore most heartily Sorry, that those Circumstances (according to the Custome & Interests of this Age, and the Satisfaction of Relations) should interrupt its farther progresse: This very Evening, as I was writing, a fit of sickness [1] Surprising me, I was faine to desist and go to bed Imediately, & this Morning hearing that Sr Sym: Harlant the Sollic^{or} was come to towne & to [1] whom my Grandson has ben just now writing, I find him (as I believed) not at all Satisfied with that Article relating to Mrs Skinner whilst for the rest there would be little to [1] regret. In all events, There are Expedients which time & providence do often produce, which cannot but render Mr Jackson as hapy as he is worthy, & as I exceedingly wish, who am S^r

Your most humble &
most faithfull Se^t
J E.

SECTION II

Finding List of Letters Advertised in Book Catalogues and in the Reports of the Historical Manuscript Commission

In the following list I have used the new style for all dates between January 1 and March 25

Evelyn to Pepys...March 14, 1667.......Davey Catalogue, 1889
——————————...September 4, 1673....Maggs Catalogue, No. 570
——————————...before item of 1680...Davey Catalogue
——————————...October, 1681........Davey Catalogue
——————————...July, 1682...........Davey Catalogue

[1] Reading doubtful.

APPENDIX

Evelyn to Pepys...March 1, 1685........Davey Catalogue
————————...June 2, 1685.........American Book Prices
                                     Current, 1930
————————...July 29, 1685........Davey Catalogue
————————...July 31, 1685........Davey Catalogue
————————...August 3, 1685......Davey Catalogue
————————...September, 1685......Davey Catalogue
————————...October 3, 1685......Davey Catalogue
————————...December, 1685......Davey Catalogue
————————...between two items   Davey Catalogue
               dated 1686.........
————————...January 2, 1686......Davey Catalogue
————————...between items, 1686...Davey Catalogue
————————...July 21, 1686........Davey Catalogue
————————...September, 1686......Davey Catalogue
————————...March 14, 1687......Davey Catalogue
————————...October, 1687........Davey Catalogue
————————...January 11, 1690.....Davey Catalogue
————————...May 30, 1694.........H. M. C. R., II, 291
————————...September 25, 1695...H. M. C. R., VI, 473
Pepys to Evelyn...January 2, 1699......Maggs Catalogue, No. 388
————————...August 1699.........Pforzheimer Collection
————————...August 1699.........Pforzheimer Collection
————————...August 19, 1700......Sotheby Catalogue, 1919

Evelyn to Pepys
[Photograph of Holograph Letter]

14 Mar:—86/7

S^r,

I was yesterday to kisse y^r hande, with y^r Historical, & Political Mercurie if you had din'd at home, and being making a step downe the River for two or three daies, I will not detaine y^r Books any Longer: I had read the last (vizt: *January*) before the former two (my Son having gotten the whole Set about a fort-night since) but I went not back to the two former months, 'til y^r Letter injoyn'd me to give you my thoughts upon them: But do you in earnest take me for such a Politician? or rather for *one,* that being lately dignifi'd of so greate an Office (as you know I have had the honour to be employ'd in) must needes have acquird an Universal Talent? I had rather Mrs Pepys should call me *Planter des Choux, herba pari*[ ] *¹iam*, Sr *Roger*—anything, than Sr *Politick*: Never-the-less, upon Condition you will hereafter put me upon some serious Subject, Such as entertain'd us th' other day, when we miss'd of hearing the Wooden-head Speake: thô I shall not adventure to *hyper-criticize*, I make this Reflection on the Reflecter, that he is now & then mistaken in his Politics; thô for the most part, I belive, more than a very shrewd Guesser: *Pag* 101 *Decemb*: *On croit que la retraite de la Cour deplusieurs grands Seigneurs d' Angleterre* etc to the End of that Paragraph, is a Super-refin'd notion upon those who have parted wth their White Slaves, but are not yet gon into ye Country, as he seemes to think:

Pag. 187 *Si le roy Jacques* etc., I should rather suppose he meant *Char: II*^{d}, for Certainly, The Martyr his Father, did not balance soe true ² the two Religions (as he pretends) *Sans pouvoir decider quelle étoit le meilleure;* Since I take him to have ben (tho' a very unfortunate prince) yet well assur'd, & firme in his perswasion, and that it was his stiffnesse (if so I may call his perseverance) which cost him his head: Is not our statesman mistaken, p. 52, *line 1, Novemb*^{r} where he makes mention of the Duke of *Ormond* etc: as well as in ye next Leafe p: 54 *Le fils naturel du Roy* etc whose mother is not at Court; tho' you guesse at the Lady he meanes? but neither is she there, nor the Mother of the young *Heroe* he speaks of: what Lapses (at this distance) there may be in his Reflections upon the other states, I pretend not to give account of; but could not passe by these without notice; and perhaps, 'twere not amisse the *Author* were advertiz'd of them: For the rest, he seemes to be a person of extraordinary penetration, and Intelligence: The *Mysteries* & *Arcana* of state are in good earnest generously comunicated, & *Nouvelles* to us *indeede,* if what he suggests in the following page 55 be the *plan* projected, & which I leave you to exercise your thoughts upon by your Selfe: The entire discourse is very hardy, as well as that 190: Dec^r: In all events We see *Louis le Grand* is to have the

¹ Letters blotted.
² Reading doubtful.

Glory of all that our wise & Valiant prince has in designe: He it is has shew'd the Way to the *Sûblime*. see: Jan: pp: 288: and 290: The whole Reflection requires your attention; add to it pp: 277. 278: But S^r, I will no longer detaine you from these curious pieces: Mithinks I am myselfe in the Cabinet, and bidding faire for a Privy Counselor, Secretary of State, Ambassador What not? Without raillery: I am extreamely delighted, and edified, and for my owne Satisfaction cannot but encourage the prosecution of a Worke, which affords so universal an Entertainement, this Inquisitive Age. We have doubtless here all that is on the Carpet of Considerable in ye Conjectures of the ablest Observer, and the publiq may learn to take their measure accordingly: In the meane while, the poore Hugenots are (I perceive) in an ill case, thô the *Fistula* should (at last) make way for the Successor: se p: 112. The Sum̄ is, that the Emperors progresse gives jealosie to the German Princes: That the *Augeburge* Combination is a trifle: that the *Swede* is to be crush'd betweene the K. of Denmark, & Poland by a Separate peace with the Turk: that Mantüa is Selling to the French, the Swisse Corrupted, & consequently Italy open'd to ye Conquerer; that *We* with *France* & the K. of *Siam* are to ruine the *Hollander* in the *Indies* & in fine, poore *Spaine* utterly forlorne & undon. *Car tel est notre boñe plaisier:* The Universal Monarch, & *Le Marquis le Louvois* has determin'd it: I am come to the end of my paper, which by my Sonne being gon with the Key of his study, & the boates staying for me & tide neere spent, makes writing on this coarse paper, irksome; And you will pardon all undecencys of this nature, & ever account of me for S^r

   Y^r most faithfull &
    most humble Servant
     J Evelyn

Before yet I quite leave ye politics, I would indeed recomend to y^r reading a shorter treatise entitled *Le Vrai Interet des Princes Chretiens* etc. pretended to be printd at *Strasbourg;* wh I think worth y^r reflection.

Evelyn to Pepys

[Photograph of Holograph Letter]

Deptford, 4th: Sep^r:—No 73

S^r,

Since my last to you of yesterday, the numbers of our Sick are So exorbitant, that even at this place, there are no lesse than 400 already cast upon us, a greate part of wch the Alle, & Victualling houses refuse to take in, because the Arrears are So greate, but those of Gravesed wh pester us most are Sent up hither upon absolute necessity, 'till my Ld. Vaughans Regiment make roome for them, which, I therefor beg of you to presse; and, as to this place, (when I foresee, I shall else be put to incredible difficulties, and to give countenance to the Employment); I intreate you to impower me, (or Deputy), to charge the Connestables with providig us quarters, in Such houses of publiq reception, as in all other places under my Care, the Lords of the Councill have already don, to the respective Mayors, Connestables & other officers; but which I have not for Deptford Towne, Greenewich nor nearer than Gravesend; because, we had no regular establishment in them, as now (I fear) we shall be forc'd to settle; unlesse this greate Arreares were in Some measure Satisfied, that the other capacious Towns might be more able, & willing to receive our men, and relieve us, who are at present so oppress'd, and continually like to grow more clamorous & troublesome, as nearer to his Mat^{ie} & ye Court: S^r, if Such a Warrant may be order'd this Bearer, sign'd by the Ld^s Comiss^{rs}: I shall know how to act & govern my Selfe, that the poore men may not lye in ye streetes: Upon Saturday next, I shall waite upon you, and receive their Lap^s farther Cōmands; my being here is in the meane time, very necessary, but a speedy Supply of monye absolut:

    S^r, I remaine
     Y^r most faithfull,
      and most humble Servant
       J Evelyn

I had received 4 lett^{rs} last night frome out of Kent; & compute ye numbers of Sick (Sent on Shore already) neare 3000—the like was never during ye former War.

APPENDIX

Evelyn to Pepys

[Copy of a portion of the letter]

[July, 1682]

". . . The tediousness of writing, and, much more, of your reading it, makes me pass by innumerable instances of the warlike exploits of Dogs amongst the Magnates, the Cimbrians, Gaules, and other fierce people, as recorded by Valorius Flaccus, Julius Pollox, Strabo, Plinie, Appion, and several more of unspotted credibility. Everybody knows how faithfully they guard the town of St. Mulos, in Bretagne, to this day, as many ages find they did a certain citty belonging to ye Romans. Nicetas Comatus tells us how, after a cruel batail fought by ye Latines against the Greeks, near Thesalonia, the citty dogs that came out for the prey would not touch the carcase of a Greek but feasted themselves upon their enemies with so strange a rabiness and appetite that they scraped them out of their graves after they had been buried. The like is also related by S—, of their distinguishing a Christian from a Turk, however disguised, and that they did notable service in the war against those miscreants. Of what considerable advantage they were, by giving intelligence of the enemy's approaches by the sagacity of their noses, historie tells us, and therefore those of Colophon trained them up for war, and formed them into companies under militarie discipline, and finding them of excellent use upon nocturnal exploits. Nay, we reade of a mighty Prince driven by his rebellious subjects out of his countrie to have been restored by the bravery of his 200 hunting dogs. . . . And it is out of Joachinium Camerarius (whichever that excellent author had it) that our Henry VIII. should send Charles V. a foot company of 400 men, who had attending on them as many stout mastives armed with iron collars, set about with sharp spikes to defend their throats, but upon what stratagem I find it not mentioned. Nor, it seems, was this the first time that British Dogs were of use upon such occasions, since we find in Strabo that they assailed the Gaules with them, and had an express officer over them appointed by imperial order. Perhaps this might be the race mentioned by our learned Camden. The more is remarkable that two great armies of the French and Swiss being on the point of joyning battle, all the dogs of the French camp leaving at once their masters, ran over to the enemy, fawning and crouching to them, which pressage the Swiss giving a fierce charge, the French gave ground, and were utterly defeated, as Paulus Jovius relates the passage. Marcus Pomponius, the Prætor, was the first we reade of who in the Sardinian war made use of dogs to find out the skulking fugitives among the rocks and fortresses, and hence the Spaniards might put in practice their late barbarities in the Western Indies. [Evelyn here relates a facetious anecdote concerning a dog belonging to 'Oveido,' but which is scarcely suitable for publication at the present day.] . . . and Le Pois tells of a soldier there who received double pay for himself and a truculent mastiff of his, which made prodigious slaughter in that war. . . . In the meantime, all we have produced as to what real service dogs may be said to have performed in the warr, 'tis certain they sometimes mistake their masters and leaders when contending with their enemies. Lions, bears, bulls, and other brutes being trained up in the same account, I find they were soon left off again, because they could not possibly discipline them to distinguish their keepers and commanders from their enemies.

> When bulls for feats of war they did array,
> Turning wild boares against their enemie;
> And Parthian lions their vaunt guard supplie,
> Under armed leaders and fierce keepers who
> Could chain and govern them: Yet vainly tho';
> For chased in fight promiscuously they slue
> Without distinction, and overthrew
> Whole legions, shaking their horrid crest;
> Nor could indeed the cavalrie resist,
> Nor rule their horse with bits, or qualifie
> Their beasts affrighted with the rabid crie;
> On each side the enraged lionesse
> Tears out the throats of such as forward presse,
> And at their back surprises 'ere aware,
> When setting loose, they pull'd them down and tare
> Them with their fangs and paws. The bull, the boar,
> Oreturned, tramples, and with his hornes did gore
> The horses in their belly and their side.
> Boars with their tusks their fellows slue and dy'd

APPENDIX 153

The scatter'd darts with blood o' the slaine, which put
In strange confusion both horse and foot

... etc. So as it seems they were faine to give over this barbarous way of fighting. My apologie for this impertinence I intend you shall have to-morrow, when I wait on you to the Morocco Indiens."

SECTION III
Finding List of Printed Letters

The reference to Braybrooke, 1825, is given where the letter is not to be found in a more modern edition. As in Section I and II of the Appendix, I am here using new style dates.

Evelyn to Pepys....January 3, 1666.......Bray, III, 329
                                         Howarth, 26
Pepys to Evelyn....February 17, 1666.....Tanner, *Further Correspondence,* 116
Evelyn to Pepys....March 26, 1666.......Bray, III, 331
                                         Howarth, 26
——————— ....March 26, 1666.......Bray, III, 332
——————— ....January 20, 1668.....Braybrooke, VI, 107
                                         Howarth, 32
Pepys to Evelyn....February 8, 1668......Braybrooke, VI, 108
                                         Howarth, 32
Evelyn to Pepys....August 21, 1669......Howarth, 35
Pepys to Evelyn....November 2, 1669....Braybrooke, VI, 112
                                         Howarth, 37
——————— ....March 1, 1667........Howarth, 66
Evelyn to Pepys....December 6, 1681.....Braybrooke, VI, 136
                                         Bray, III, 406
                                         Tanner, I, 14
                                         Howarth, 119
——————— .... April 28, 1682........Braybrooke, VI, 139
                                         Tanner, I, 21
                                         Howarth, 129

Evelyn to Pepys	June 5, 1682	Howarth, 144
———	September 19, 1682	Bray III, 414
Pepys to Evelyn	August 7, 1683	Howarth, 151
Evelyn to Pepys	August 10, 1683	Howarth, 152
———	June 8, 1684	Tanner, I, 23
———	September 23, 1685	Bray, III, 420
Pepys to Evelyn	October 2, 1685	Bray, III, 422
		Howarth, 169
Evelyn to Pepys	March 1, 1688	Howarth, 186
Pepys to Evelyn	September 10, 1688	Howarth, 193
Evelyn to Pepys	December 12, 1688	Braybrooke, VI, 163
		Howarth, 198
———	May 10, 1689	Braybrooke (1825), II, 108
———	August 12, 1689	Bray, III, 435
Pepys to Evelyn	August 30, 1689	Bray, III, 457
		Howarth, 204
Evelyn to Pepys	October 4, 1689	Bray, III, 458
		Howarth, 205
———	June 11, 1690	Tanner, I, 29
		Howarth, 215
———	August 14, 1690	Braybrooke, VI, 168
		Tanner, I, 33
		Howarth, 218
———	September 25, 1690	Braybrooke (1825), II, 112
Pepys to Evelyn	September 25, 1690	Howarth, 218
Evelyn to Pepys	September 26, 1690	Braybrooke, VI, 169
		Tanner, I, 33
		Howarth, 219
Pepys to Evelyn	November 13, 1690	Howarth, 222
———	October 8, 1691	Howarth, 223
———	January 9, 1692	Braybrooke, VI, 172
		Tanner, I, 51
		Howarth, 226
———	March 28, 1692	Braybrooke, VI, 173
		Tanner, I, 56
		Howarth, 227

APPENDIX

Evelyn to Pepys.... August 29, 1692....... Braybrooke, VI, 175
                                            Tanner, I, 59
                                            Howarth, 229
Pepys to Evelyn.... September 16, 1692.... Tanner, I, 62
                                            Howarth, 232
Evelyn to Pepys.... July 6, 1693.......... Tanner, I, 67
Pepys to Evelyn..... May 22, 1694......... Howarth, 240
Evelyn to Pepys.... July 7, 1694.......... Tanner, I, 94
                                            Howarth, 241
Pepys to Evelyn.... August 10, 1694...... Tanner, I, 96
                                            Howarth, 246
Evelyn to Pepys.... September 2, 1694.... Tanner, I, 99
                                            Howarth, 248
Pepys to Evelyn.... November 7, 1694..... Howarth, 252
Evelyn to Pepys.... November 18, 1694.... Tanner, I, 102
                                            Howarth, 253
————————————.... December 3, 1696... Tanner, I, 133
                                            Howarth, 265
————————————.... January 14, 1699..... Howarth, 271
————————————.... May 10, 1700........ Braybrooke, VI, 221
                                            Howarth, 298
————————————.... May 18, 1700......... Tanner, I, 342
                                            Howarth, 300
————————————.... July 22, 1700........ Tanner, II, 19
                                            Howarth, 302
Pepys to Evelyn..... August 7, 1700...... Braybrooke, VI, 225
                                            Tanner, II, 35
                                            Howarth, 305
Evelyn to Pepys.... August 9, 1700....... Tanner, II, 38
                                            Howarth, 306
————————————.... August 25, 1700....... Tanner, II, 50
                                            Howarth, 307
Pepys to Evelyn.... September 19, 1700.... Tanner, II, 72
                                            Howarth, 309
————————————.... June 7, 1701.......... Howarth, 332
————————————.... November 19, 1701.... Howarth, 334

Evelyn to Pepys.... December 10, 1701.... Tanner, II, 237
Howarth, 335
Pepys to Evelyn.... December 24, 1701.... Braybrooke, VI, 234
Tanner, II, 241
Howarth, 328
Evelyn to Pepys.... January 20, 1703...... Braybrooke, VI, 252
Tanner, II, 298
Howarth, 369